Special Praise for *The Gift of Fulfillment*

"In the area of addiction recovery and the important intersection of that recovery in relation to Christian principles, Michael Dinneen's new book is required reading."

—Philip F. Anschutz, Philanthropist, Entrepreneur

"*The Gift of Fulfillment* is based on the notion that a human being is born with a 'hole within,' which leads to feelings of emptiness, dissatisfaction, and sadness. Michael Dinneen's work with people who find themselves hurting and dissatisfied is intensely practical and makes it possible to gain a sense of direction, serenity, and purpose. Michael has a passion and commitment to bridge the world of recovery with the Christian world without excluding other points of view. *The Gift of Fulfillment* deserves your attention."

—Bob Buford, Founder, Leadership Network,
Author of *Halftime* and *Finishing Well*

"As one committed to the human journey with God, I am pleased to endorse Michael Dinneen's effort to bring practical clarity to the miracle of recovery, when God becomes the Center of the human heart. He captures well the call to 'become the change you wish to see in others.'"

—Richard C. Hanifen, Bishop Emeritus of the Roman
Catholic Diocese of Colorado Springs

The Gift

of

Fulfillment

The Gift
of
Fulfillment

LIVING *the* PRINCIPLES
of HEALTHY RECOVERY

MICHAEL DINNEEN

CENTRAL RECOVERY PRESS

Las Vegas

Central Recovery Press (CRP) is committed to publishing exceptional materials addressing addiction treatment, recovery, and behavioral healthcare topics, including original and quality books, audio/visual communications, and web-based new media. Through a diverse selection of titles, we seek to contribute a broad range of unique resources for professionals, recovering individuals and their families, and the general public.

For more information, visit www.centralrecoverypress.com.

Publisher: Central Recovery Press
            3321 N. Buffalo Drive
            Las Vegas, NV 89129

18 17 16 15 14 13   1 2 3 4 5

ISBN: 978-1-937612-31-3 (paper)
      978-1-937612-32-0 (e-book)

Photo of Michael Dinneen by Don Weule. Used with permission.

Publisher's Note: Our books represent the experiences and opinions of their authors only. Every effort has been made to ensure that events, institutions, and statistics presented in our books as facts are accurate and up-to-date.

To protect their privacy, the names of some of the people and institutions in this book have been changed.

Cover and Interior Design by Deb Tremper, Six Penny Graphics.

To Mom and Dad,
and Uncle Tom.
Thank you for everything.

Table of Contents

Acknowledgments

First and most importantly I want to thank my God (Father, Son, and Holy Spirit) for everything. I thank my beautiful wife Jill and my amazing children, Cadin and Samantha, for loving me through the process of writing my first book. I thank my sister Jennifer for guiding me to my first twelve-step meeting more than twenty-one years ago. I have gratitude for all the participants in the thousands of recovery meetings that I've had the privilege to attend. Thanks to Helen O'Reilly, Eliza Tutellier, and all the CRP staff for their guidance. Thanks to Walden Media and Todd Neff for helping me edit and organize my proposal. I have deep gratitude to Phil Anschutz for his vision and funding of CeDAR as well as all his help with this project. Thanks to all the CeDAR staff who have been so supportive.

Thanks to friends like Brett Kessler, Dan Griffen, Robert Soto, David Kiser, Shaun Collins, and Charles, who encouraged me along over the past year. Thanks to Rev. Bill Connors for his life-giving message and friendship as well as the support I've received from my church community group. Thanks to all the patients I've been privileged to serve at CeDAR, especially Dave G, Jeff C, and John M. Thanks so much to all my mentors, sponsees, friends, and family. Thanks to Joe Arington for providing me the computer on which to write the book. Thanks to Jodi, Bill, and Marilyn for the pre-edits. I want to thank Dennis for being a great friend and mentor for the past twenty-two years.

Lastly, thanks to all the incredible people quoted throughout these pages who have impacted my life in a positive way.

Introduction

The Gift of Fulfillment is based on the notion that a human being is born with—or develops over time—a "hole" within that is characterized by feelings of emptiness, dissatisfaction, and sadness. Some of us try to fill this hole with anything from food, money, power, prestige, alcohol, drugs, or entertainment, to religion, work, physical fitness, material consumption, people, sex, TV, fantasy, and so forth. Some of these "fillers" may be good in moderation, but they fail to *fully satisfy* us. They do not bring us the peace or happiness, the intimacy or sense of connection that we yearn for. After trying for years to fill these holes, people become unhappy and increasingly depressed about their circumstances. They cling to the belief that if things were only different on the "outside," they would feel differently on the "inside."

This book is a guide for readers who seek to address this void within in a very practical and satisfying way. Its approach is based on the spiritual tools used in twelve-step recovery circles to overcome addiction. With these tools it's possible to gain a sense of direction, serenity, and purpose: They are a course in Life 101. The twelve-step tenets apply to anyone who has problems—which is everyone.

I am a wounded person who has been given the miracle of internal and external transformation over the last twenty-two years. The process of healing and becoming my true self will never be totally complete, but

I am the happiest and most connected to God that I have ever been. Throughout most of my life I was tortured by some form of addiction, some obsession, or feelings of inadequacy. I had a major sensitivity to criticism and I depended on sources outside of myself to give me a sense of security and self-worth. I am not cured of my weaknesses, but when I apply the principles outlined in this book, I am able to use my past failures and current struggles for good.

As a confused twenty-three-year-old I was granted the gift of desperation, which has led to the gift of fulfillment. I was a reckless, lonely, and fearful prodigal son who got a second chance at life after I called out for help with my heart. As I will explain, I believe that God got me into the twelve-step recovery movement so that the twelve-step recovery movement, in turn, could get me to God. I want to share this process with anyone who will listen and who feels that there is room for growth within themselves. I believe that the spiritual principles embodied in the Twelve Steps of addiction recovery can help anyone.

Essentially, the Twelve Steps help us take "the plank out of our own eye," as Jesus advised, and see life clearly. When I see others, the world, and myself more accurately, I am able to experience forgiveness and a true sense of purpose.

The Gift of Fulfillment presents a simple—if not an easy—plan. People need inspiration to get the process started, to stick with it and see it implemented. As we say in the twelve-step world, "Quitting (substances/behaviors) is not our problem; it is staying quit that is the issue." Similarly, for people who do not suffer from addiction, but who nevertheless feel a void in their lives, starting a life that leads to true fulfillment is not the problem; it is sticking with it that is the issue.

I was given a way to live that becomes more and more gratifying as time goes on. It all starts with admitting the truth about ourselves at the deepest level—the level of the heart. As painful as the truth can be, it is a gift. Through the help of others it is my hope that you will begin to observe the flaws in your thinking, to become open-minded to a spiritual way of living, and to gain hope for yourself and this world. Hopefully, you are in enough pain that there is a willingness to take direction from a mentor, to join a community of (admittedly, since we *all* are) imperfect people, and to surrender. Over time you can (if you wish) develop a reliance on, and a friendship with, the ultimate source of love and power. Although at times you may desire to revert to your old way of living, seeking and accepting God's love can become your true joy.

As you grow, you begin to discover that "You are not a bad person trying to get good; you are a sick person trying to get well." I am offering suggestions to aid you in a process of introspection that will lead you into the wilderness of your inner being. It is essential to be willing to identify the elements blocking you from happiness, and to be equally willing to do whatever it takes to be free.

When this process takes root inside of an individual, he or she begins to feel much more comfortable within. There will be much less comparing and less judgment of self and others. When that occurs, people stop wanting to alter themselves in some form or another to escape reality. Throughout this journey your strengths and weaknesses will be refined. With the practice of the spiritual principles you develop true empathy for others as self-centeredness diminishes. People who want even more freedom will try to make things right with the people they have hurt over time. Thus, to the best of your ability and with a lot of grace, you get right with God, yourself, and the world.

Then, if you choose to move forward with this way of life, you will enter the growth phase of spiritual development. There will be constant opportunities to grow and change through self-analysis, prayer and meditation, and through learning how to serve others. The natural by-product of the process will be for you to freely give to those around you what you have been freely given. There are constant opportunities to practice the art of admitting when you are wrong, and of being mindful of your thoughts and emotions. An understanding develops that you are becoming who you were always meant to be—and that will give you a sense of serenity you never knew before. Obviously, as humans we continue to experience many struggles, but a different perspective about life's difficulties can emerge within you, and this makes all the difference.

As I practice the principles outlined in this book, my life may not look overly exciting (on paper). I go to recovery meetings and mentor others, I spend time with my wife and kids, participate in a church community, exercise, and work as a team leader at a hospital's addictions program. I enjoy various outdoor sports, spend time with friends, travel, visit family, laugh, cry, and try to do and be in harmony with God's will for me (which is so much better than what I had ever imagined). It is my internal world that is unexplainable. I now have the capacity to love, and every day I grow in my ability to be in greater communion with the world around me.

There are no new ideas or principles in this book, because these spiritual truths are universal, just as physical laws are universal. I have certainly benefited a great deal from my church, from good therapy, education, and physical fitness—but in this book I want to focus on basic twelve-step spirituality. I will take you through a universally applicable process that can help with any of life's problems.

I hope this book finds its way to people who want something different for themselves but do not know where to start. I hope to encourage you to begin to live a life that will lead to a true sense of purpose and fulfillment. I hope this book finds its way into the hands of the broken people who need to know that they can find their true purpose, their own gift of fulfillment, if only they are willing to seek, ask for help, and follow direction.

CHAPTER ONE
The Process

> *"There is no chance, no destiny, no fate, that can hinder or control the firm resolve of a determined soul."*
>
> —Ella Wheeler Wilcox

I believe our hearts yearn to experience the love of God. Our souls long for union with God's love. To give and receive love is the answer to the void or emptiness inside each of us.

I have a friend named Brent who understands the void. He is a dentist in recovery from addiction. He and I give workshops for dentists and dental office staff on the topics of meth mouth (advanced tooth decay attributed to meth use), addiction, and intervention. A couple of years ago we were on a four-hour drive to one of our gigs. As we chatted, we first checked in with each other about our lives, and planned some future outdoor sporting adventures. We began to talk about the message of personal transformation we had experienced and that we believe we had been given in order to share. The conversation centered on the addiction recovery effort and on how the principles embodied in recovery are universal and can easily be used by everyone who seeks a serious life change.

For example, Brent himself rose from being an addict to being a person running a successful dental practice. He helps recovering individuals get dental work they cannot afford but which they desperately need in order to become employable, productive members of society. He is also a triathlete coach, a faithful, loving husband, and father to four wonderful kids. He has a great sense of humor, really enjoys his life, and yet he is still very much human. He is still working through issues after more than a decade of good recovery. He has excellent mentors and good friends and a life program that works—especially during the tough times that always come in life. Brent has consistently applied certain principles and actions in his life that have resulted in a sense of peace, happiness, and direction that he had never known before. The most important aspect of his life is his connection with God. I believe any person committed to a similar program and approach can achieve the passion for life that Brent and I experience.

This is why I wrote this book—to bring the principles of twelve-step recovery to people who might not otherwise have reason to find them; people who are not addicts, but who find themselves hurting and dissatisfied with fruitless attempts to fill their spiritual voids from without, rather than from within.

I hope that those who read this book and apply the principles and suggestions of the Twelve Steps to their own lives will find the same spiritual connection, happiness, and fulfillment that my friend Brent and I and millions of others have found.

The book is a collection of real people's experiences that illustrate the principles of true spiritual awakening and personality transformation. It can be used as a "how-to" guide for anyone ready for a different way of living and thinking. In short, this is the process of giving up, cleaning up, making up, and growing up. Yes, it is the process used in twelve-step recovery. Yes, it will work for you, too, even if you are not an addict (in the traditional sense).

Currently, I work at an addiction treatment center that also treats co-occurring disorders, such as depression and anxiety. We are part of a large medical center and operate one of the most intense treatment experiences in the world. I supervise the extended-care sixty-day residential program and the professionals' program. I also get to do weekly workshops with the patients on spiritual development, and I carry a caseload. In addition, I work with some clients and families if there are sexual issues or continuing care issues that require my expertise.

Because we are a teaching hospital, we have many observers and interns, fellows, residents, and nursing students. Many professionals in the recovery community agree that the principles we use in our treatment program—especially the twelve-step process originally developed by Bill Wilson, Dr. Bob Smith, and the other founding members of Alcoholics Anonymous—could benefit anyone who is seeking to resolve life's pains and problems. My approach is based on personal experiences as well as my extensive observations of twelve-step recovery. The following twelve-step spiritual principles are generally recognized as those embedded in the steps of recovery:

- honesty
- hope
- faith
- trust
- courage
- integrity
- willingness
- humility
- brotherly love
- justice
- perseverance
- service

I believe that the only way we can effectively adopt these principles as a way of life is by being part of a supportive community that fosters true fellowship and mentorship (or, as it is called in recovery, "sponsorship"). For the purposes of this book, I will use the terms "mentor" and "sponsor" interchangeably.

The following chapters will guide you to address the void within in a down-to-earth and rewarding way, relying on spiritual tools with which to build a sense of direction, serenity, and purpose. This is a broad path that leads to true fulfillment. I invite you to walk it with me.

The first step is to identify your problems and to admit to them. After that, it is important to become part of a community and learn the value of mentorship. There is an opportunity to learn to live by the principles of honesty, open-mindedness, and willingness. There are suggestions on how to implement the tasks of creating a personal inventory, living a life of transparency, and making restitution for harms done. I will provide tools for daily living to help you continually grow in your effectiveness and powers of perception. Prayer and meditation may become essential elements in your journey, and living a life of service can become the source of your joy and happiness. Finally, you may begin to understand one of life's greatest paradoxes: In order to truly gain a new life, we must first experience the death of our old one.

I will argue that acquiring the capacity for happiness is a by-product of right living. As the neurologist, psychiatrist, and Holocaust survivor Viktor Frankl wrote: "Success, like happiness, cannot be pursued; it must ensue . . . as the unintended side-effect of one's personal dedication to a cause greater than oneself." If you adhere to the tenets presented in this book, I believe you will experience profoundly positive life changes. Certainly, some people with severe or co-occurring issues may still require professional support and services. But the approaches presented here will be helpful to you nonetheless, and may even revolutionize your life.

The solution I propose is spiritual, but also very practical. By incorporating a broad, all-inclusive spiritual process of healing, you can move from a self-centered prison to a life of joy and freedom. How do I know this? Because of my own life experience and because of the experiences of the many people I have had the privilege of associating with over the past twenty-two years. I will show you what steps to take, and how. I have adapted techniques used personally and with my patients, the so-called "twelve-step process," because I believe it can help all kinds of people—not only people who are struggling to recover from addiction—to lead happier, more productive, and more meaningful lives.

Hitting Bottom or Raising the Bottom

The journey to the true self seems to usually start with some form of pain. I have heard it referred to as the "Gift of Desperation." It is characterized by a sense of deep acceptance or awareness about your own condition that goes far beyond what words can adequately describe.

The internal change begins with the admission of the truth. That is why each addict in a twelve-step meeting introduces him- or herself with the words, "Hello, my name is . . . , and I'm an addict." It is an admission of the truth about oneself and an acceptance of the facts. It is a miraculous movement of information from head to heart (from intellectualization to emotional internalization). It cannot be explained in words. But I have seen it manifest in many people.

Examples of the shift from head knowledge to heart knowledge are all around us; take the case of nutrition information. We have known for many years that obesity leads to problems like high blood pressure, back pain, and shortness of breath. It may even contribute to heart disease or stroke. We know how we should eat in order to maintain a healthy weight. We know it, but how many of us wait until we have a mild heart attack or a stroke before we act? Head knowledge has to become heart awareness before we "sit up and take notice."

As I stated in the Introduction, I was twenty-three when I hit bottom. It was August of 1991, and I was working for a computer company in Hopkinton, Massachusetts, after graduating from Boston College in 1990. I went on a serious bender and disappeared from work. I came out of a blackout on a ferryboat going to Nantucket Island, having a few more drinks with some drinking buddies. As we were pulling into Nantucket Harbor, I determined that waiting for hundreds of people to disembark was a poor use of my time. Why not simply jump off the ship? Embarrassed at the size of my beer belly,

I decided to leave my shirt on and hand my shoes and wallet to a friend. I jumped over the top railing.

When I was arrested on shore, the police asked me if I was suicidal. I answered, "Nope, just impatient." They put me in jail, processed me, and told me to come back for court on Monday. The night before the hearing, a couple of my buddies and I met some people at a bar, followed by a party in our hotel room. That Sunday night I remember sitting in bed, evidence of debauchery all around me, and having a deep realization—a moment of clarity—that I was not a normal guy. There was something wrong with me. I tried to imagine what normal guys did when they were on this resort island. Maybe they were on sailboats drinking champagne, gazing at the stars with their wives, strolling down cobblestone streets, attending art shows or church functions. But I could not visualize myself doing any of those things. I could not see myself living a normal life. I could not imagine any kind of life for myself other than the life of dissolution I was living; I could not see any way out.

Once back on the mainland, however, I was to have a moment of grace while a friend was driving me home along Route 9 in Boston. I had not been back to the office yet—I did not know if I had a job to go back to. But I had a moment of total surrender and acceptance. In the past, I always had a plan for how I was going to change my life. I was an Irish Catholic kid from New York with an addicted brain and a distorted view of God. I had an image of God as some large, bearded, old white guy who maybe looked like Zeus, up in the sky watching my every move. I figured He was not very happy with me. I had a lot of shame, a lot of guilt, a lot of self-hatred, a lot of fear, and a lot of remorse. I had stopped praying. I thought if I prayed, God would know where I was, and if God knew where I was, he would take me out with a Zeus-like thunderbolt.

I would tell myself, "Well, I'm going to move to a different place, I'm going to get a new job, I'm going to quit smoking, I'm going to start doing push-ups and sit-ups and get in good shape. It's time for the big change to happen." I would write all these things down, yet a few days later I was back to my old ways.

This time something was different. My friend and I were driving along in a Jeep with no top and a busted rearview mirror. It was chilly. I was hungover, badly sunburned, and shivering in the chilly Massachusetts night. I was wondering where my life was going and worrying whether I was going to be fired for not showing up at work. I was too scared and overwhelmed to speak. Everything became dark and depressing. There was no way out. I could not imagine my life continuing the way it was and yet I could not imagine my life being any different.

I was fed up. Everywhere I went I eventually hurt people, cheated on girlfriends, worried my mother sick, embarrassed my sister, or otherwise got in trouble. I would hurt friendships because I could not be trusted. The list of my shortcomings went on and on and as I became aware of them, I broke down.

At that precise instant, I did not care if I lived or died. I called out to God in that moment; not with words, but in my heart. In the past, it had been "Hail Mary full of grace, help me find a parking space," or a foxhole-type of prayer. You know the kind: "Get me out of this and I will be a good boy." But this time it was simply, "Help me. I am hopeless."

A sense of peace came over me. I knew then that I was an addict. And I knew that I was going to be okay. I was overwhelmed by a strong sense of what I would call the Spirit of the Universe. I knew with every cell in my body that everything in the universe was exactly the way it was supposed to be. That moment, in the Jeep rolling down Route 9, was rock bottom, my moment of truth, my acceptance, and my surrender wrapped into one experience. I had been bumped into spiritual kindergarten and thus my journey began. I thought my life was over, when actually it was just beginning. There was much work and much healing to be accomplished.

The experience of "hitting bottom" is different for everyone. Not everyone has a "burning bush" or a "white light" experience. Some people just become "sick and tired of being sick and tired." Others are forced to look at their issues due to an intervention by family, friends, employers, doctors, or lawyers. How you get on the path to true fulfillment does not matter. What matters is that you get on the path and give it an honest try.

Accepting the Truth and Being Honest with Yourself

The ability of the human mind and the ego to lie to itself is amazing. A friend of mine says, "A broken car cannot fix itself, and neither can a broken mind." We are all broken to a certain degree because we are human, and that is part of the human experience. Brokenness is not the problem. The problem is that most of us have no idea how broken we actually are, or how beautiful we actually are. Most of us have a perception problem. We do not see the truth about ourselves or the world around us.

So it is vitally important that you make a commitment to seeking the truth about your circumstances. The beginning of the solution is being honest with yourself or letting someone help you see the truth. It can start with a simple admission of how you are thinking or feeling.

"I'm anxious most of the time."

"I'm not happy in my marriage."

"I hate my job. I'm dissatisfied in my career."

"I can't seem to control my drinking or substance use."

"I can't quit smoking."

"I have an anger and fear problem."

"I can never make enough money—I always want more."

"I feel deep shame and self-hatred over my excessive pornography use and the time I spend in Internet chat rooms, but I continue to act out."

"If people just acted differently then things would be better."

"I feel depressed and sad about my life and relationships."

"I'm not the person I want to be."

"I care too much about what everyone thinks of me."

"I have issues with eating and food."

"I have everything anyone could want, but I'm still unhappy."

"I vow to do things differently but I don't stick with it."

"I can't seem to get out of debt."

"I hate my boss and I don't like my coworkers."

"I'm saddened by the fact that I cannot find true love."

"I don't feel connected or accepted at my church."

"I feel hopeless."

"These medications are becoming a problem."

"I am working all the time."

"I am always stressed-out."

"I live with a sense of loneliness."

"I am insecure about my abilities."

"It feels like my anger gets triggered out of nowhere."

"This is not the life I thought I would have."

"I am terrified of failure."

"I am desperate for her love and acceptance."

"I have lost my sense of self by compulsively giving to others."

"I am obsessed with my attempts at achieving more success."

"I feel depressed and anxious."

The list is endless. As unlikely as this may seem to you while you are in pain, the problems that you think you have can turn out to be blessings, because they are the reasons you open up to an incredible transformation of your heart and soul. The journey will be under way when you can honestly say, "I need help and I cannot fix myself with my own willpower." When I work with patients in recovery, I acknowledge their pain. But I also show them they can leave their misery behind.

I have heard it said, "Try this new way of life that I will describe for ninety days, and if you are not completely satisfied then I will gladly refund all of your misery!" Even better—I've seen it come to pass.

I believe there is a better, more gratifying, and spiritually healthier way to change and resolve the majority of life's issues. It all starts with being honest with yourself and accepting your present circumstances. The self-honesty begins with admitting your problems (or your perception of the issues that are affecting you). The process of healing begins with your acceptance of the truth. In Chapter Two, I will give a few assignments to help facilitate the internalization of these concepts and break down denial (defined as when you do not admit, even to yourself, that you are lying). For now, please take a journal and write about what you hope to receive from reading this book. Write about your life and what you are seeking. What do you believe are your problems? What are you willing to do to find serenity, healing, and fulfillment? Remember that you do not have to be an addict to benefit from the method of working the Twelve Steps that I describe.

Please do not skip these mini assignments. What this book offers—hope and healing—is found only to the degree to which you are committed to the process. This whole book is about your willingness to take action and to open your mind to spiritual principles.

Open-mindedness and Hope

When you gain clarity and accept the truth about yourself, you face the next challenge: being open-minded. At this point in the process, you need to be open-minded about what can help you with your problems and issues, your thinking, and your actions. Recognizing and addressing the distortions of your thoughts and actions are processes, not events. The two big indicators that you are ready to engage in this part of the process are, one, that you can say, "Maybe something or someone can help me" and, two, "There is hope."

One example in my own life that illustrates a small part of this stage happened in 1992. My computer company had relocated me to Colorado and I did not have any solid connections to new friends, a community, my God, or myself. I was constantly feeling shame and self-hatred, which I later realized were other forms of self-obsession.

I recall shooting hoops by myself one evening, feeling quite despondent about my life and circumstances. I had recently seen a documentary about John Newton, the man who wrote the song "Amazing Grace." Newton had been involved in the slave trade in the 1700s, but later he had a spiritual conversion. Over time he became a totally different man; he eventually became an Anglican clergyman, and it was this experience that is reflected in the lyrics of the beautiful hymn, "I once was lost, but now am found, was blind, but now I see."

At that moment of sadness, I thought about Newton. I realized that if he could change (or be changed by God), then maybe there was some hope for me, too. If there was actually a Creator or Divine Presence in the universe that was full of power and love, then what was it that made me so sick or defective that I couldn't be helped? I realized that if God created everything in the universe, then He would be okay with me exploring everything I could in order to discover Him, including religion, nature, etc. Little did I know that God was actually pursuing me.

This moment of clear thinking was a solid step forward in my long process of rebuilding my sense of self and my sense of hope. It took many more such moments to help me through the initial process, and these types of experiences would happen to me again and again as I continued to seek healing and answers. I have heard thousands of variations on these types of stories and the internal processes they represent. I will write about a few of them, as well as discuss the principles of willingness and surrender.

The Willingness to Let Go of Control

Giving in to change makes many, maybe most, people feel uncomfortable. Only when our "pain level" rises higher than our "fear level" do most of us become willing to give up control and embrace change. I will tell you a secret: Control is only an illusion, anyway. I promise you, the magic of change will start to happen when you relinquish the illusion of control.

A few years ago, for Mother's Day, my sister took my mother to New York City for what they called a "Weekend with Oprah." They later told me a great story that Oprah had told the studio audience about her own life. Apparently, before her career took off, her life's dream was to be in the movie *The Color Purple*. She auditioned for the movie but did not hear back from anyone.

Oprah checked into a center to help her with her weight loss and eating habits. As she was exercising, running around a track by herself, she completely surrendered the movie dream to God from her heart. At that moment, somebody yelled to her that Steven Spielberg's assistant was on the phone. He offered her a part in the movie! With no acting experience, she received an Academy Award nomination. And her career took off.

Community, Mentorship, and True Friendship

The most important thing I have ever learned is that I cannot do this thing we call life on my own. Reading spiritual material, contemplation, prayer, and solitude are critical elements of the spiritual life, but my Creator also seems to reach me through community, friendships, and mentors. The process that I will describe needs to happen with a group of like-minded people who can encourage and share their own experience, strength, and hope with you along the way. This book will explore where to find such a group for yourself, and how to engage a mentor. When the student is ready, the teacher will appear. Do you think you are ready?

Chip was a friend of mine who helped start an organization called Phoenix Multisport, which fosters a healthy community of various daily activities and friendships as an alternative to drug use. He has a great personality and an active life, but he is not without his share of pain. He lost his brother and sister-in-law and ended up adopting their three little kids, one of whom has serious special needs.

Years ago Chip's life had spiraled out of control and he began the journey of practicing the spiritual principles embodied in this book. He made a couple of good friends who were also attempting to change their lives for the better and he developed a strong sense of brotherhood with these men. When Chip became a father overnight and was overwhelmed, one of these friends faithfully showed up every Thursday night to babysit so that Chip could spend a couple of hours with his mourning wife, who had, after all, lost her brother. They were overwhelmed by their new responsibilities as parents, and they needed time to reconnect with each other and take care of themselves.

When asked about friendship, Chip spoke about the importance of time. He feels it is essential not to give to your friends in your spare time, but to make them a priority, sometimes putting them in front of your own perceived needs. For instance, when his good friend and mentor was going through a divorce, Chip jumped on a plane and spent a few days walking and talking with him. He said, "If we want someone to do it for us, then we had better be prepared to do it for others."

Getting Right with Yourself

A rabbi friend talks about a man named Yisroel Salanter who lived in
the late 1800s. Salanter was also a rabbi, or teacher, "who believed that
people need to analyze themselves on a daily basis, and that man's purpose
in this world is to change his character for the good." *Shvirat* (to break)
hamidot (one's character). The chapter on resentment, fear, and relationship
inventories will lead you to insights about your character flaws. To begin
to get right with yourself, you need to delve deeply beneath the symptoms
(chemicals, behaviors, depression, discontentment, etc.) in search of the
true cause. As Leo Tolstoy so aptly stated: "Everyone thinks of changing the
world, but no one thinks of changing himself."

What produces the symptoms that make you feel the need to alter yourself
or escape reality? The healing journey of getting right with yourself
involves uncovering the things that are blocking you from your peace
and self-acceptance. The inventory process I will outline involves dealing
with resentments, hurt, shame, guilt, secrets, personality traits, fears,
relationships, and sex issues. You will identify your true assets and liabilities
and see yourself clearly. The truth will set you free—but first it will piss you
off! It is an uncomfortable process, but one that pays huge dividends.

As you work to identify the things inside of you that block you from your
Creator and your true self, you will begin to experience yourself as you were
always meant to be. When you tap into this aspect of yourself, you realize
that a big part of your peace and contentment comes from getting right
with yourself (and your Higher Power). Remember what Socrates said:
"The unexamined life is not worth living." The inventory process is self-
examination.

Transparency, Humility, and Character Development

In the twelve-step programs that are a part of my life and the lives of my
patients, the next step after completing an inventory is to share the results
with a trusted mentor who understands this process and will be supportive
of you. A later chapter will be dedicated to the topics of transparency,
humility, and character development.

Many people fear this type of honest disclosure. They think it will unveil "the impostor" they believe really lives within them. I, too, felt this sense of being an impostor for many years. When a supervisor would ask to see me in his or her office, I would think, "Uh-oh, what do they know?" As if there was anything to know.

Deep down inside, most people hold the conscious or unconscious thought, "If you really knew all of my thoughts, feelings, and past actions, you would not like, love, or accept me." This is a huge lie! After full disclosure is completed, there is usually a great sense of relief. You can now have the knowledge and acceptance that you are doing the best you can. You can develop a healthy confidence that you belong, and that you are no better or worse than anyone else.

Next, there will be a task to help you identify character issues that need improvement. The process begins by addressing the major issues in your life, which will lead to the underlying character flaws that need to be identified, revealed, and healed. These character issues are the obstacles to your overall serenity, effectiveness, and connection with others. By this time in the process, a healthy degree of humility may be the gift you experience. The goal is to become "right-sized," a process that lasts a lifetime. I like the definition that says, "Humility is not thinking less of yourself, it is thinking of yourself less."

Getting Right with the World

Eventually, you will learn how to go about making things right with the world and with yourself. You can attempt to repair what you have done to others by making amends in whatever way you can to those you have harmed. Instead of focusing your attention on the harms the world has done to you, you will focus on your part in inflicting harm. This is where all the work really starts to pay off. In making right the wrongs you have done to others, you will win a dose of serenity and a sense of purpose that will change your entire outlook on life.

For instance, Patrick, a man from one of my groups, made amends to his daughter. He sat down with her and told her he had mistreated her by not being present, that he'd broken her trust, that he'd failed her in any number of ways. He got to a point where he asked her, "Is there anything that you want to say?" The daughter didn't let him off the hook. "Yes, Daddy, you did do all those things," she said.

"What can I do to make it right?" he asked.

"You can play with me, Daddy," she answered. "You can spend more time with me."

And she crawled up onto his lap, started to cry, and hugged him. At this moment of embrace, there was nothing but healing and love between these two family members. Patrick's wife, who didn't quite trust her husband yet, witnessed it all. She said it was the most powerful thing she had ever seen in her life.

I have a friend who says that it was important for her to make amends to herself. She found that the compassion that we are seeking to develop for others needs to be extended to ourselves if we are to heal. It may sound like therapeutic malarkey, but there really is a child inside all of us whom we need to nurture, protect, and befriend.

Growing Up

The amends process needs to be followed by yet more action. After the process is complete, you will learn to live with the goal of love and tolerance for others. Learning how to live without creating emotional hangovers and starting to create emotional balance is wonderful. I will make suggestions on how to progress by doing short daily inventories to keep your spiritual connection—a priceless gift in itself. Just like physical exercise, you need to train consistently in order to stay sharp and make progress.

I remember a few years ago when I needed to get a new hospital badge at work. The woman in the identification office was late for the appointment and was rude to me. I had a sense of superiority, and, I admit, I was a jerk to her. Afterward, as I walked across the parking lot back to my office, I felt proud and told myself that I would email her boss and tell him about the poor customer service I had received. I kept rehearsing the scene over in my mind and feeling justified each time.

But before I could send the email, I spoke with a friend who called me a few choice names because of my attitude of entitlement. I realized he was right. I realized that what was said in so many rooms of recovery was and is true: "If you spot it, then you got it." It wasn't the woman's attitude that was the problem; it was my own (and, regardless, mine was the only one I could change). I knew that I needed to make amends to the woman for my behavior, so I walked back over to her office and told her that she had a difficult job and that I was sorry for being rude to her. My talk with my friend had helped me realize that the woman's rudeness was obvious to me, because I have the same capacity for rudeness within myself. We forgave each other and she seemed deeply affected. I was able to move ahead with my day without carrying negative thoughts. In fact, I emailed her supervisor and told him that I thought she was doing good work. I needed to get right with her for my own spiritual connection. I find myself admitting to my wife and kids that "I was wrong" about something every week.

We need to be willing to admit it when we are wrong, do what we can to make things right, and stay clean inside so we can stay connected to God. Doing so will become part of our lifestyle.

Prayer and Meditation

I believe I make progress by learning how to improve my connection with my God through prayer and meditation. There are many ways to pray and meditate. Each person's journey is unique. You need power in your life to sustain a sense of direction and purpose. The fruit of this never-ending process involves true, deep connections with life itself, which by extension involves embracing the very thing you may have been running from: intimacy with God. We are all left wanting more in life because we are going to the wrong sources to fill our emptiness. Your Creator is the only source that can give you what you really want. Once we are filled by the right source, we make fewer demands on ourselves and our friends, family, employers, and so on. For example, we can accept our spouses for who they are instead of trying to change them for our own happiness.

You may come to acknowledge that you have been trying to fill your spiritual hole with chemicals, people, sex, or money and material things, status, and entertainment. When these things become mini gods to us, it is high time to reprioritize and put them back into perspective. Unless we have a better option we will keep going back to the old ways, only to get the same unsatisfying results. Tapping into God's love for you and accessing His power is the only thing that truly satisfies.

I have had the privilege of mentoring a doctor named Garret for the past few years. He faithfully attends his recovery meetings as well as church. He has gone through many challenges in his marriage as well as with his four sons. He believes that prayer has carried him through all of the tough times. He says that a constant conscious contact with God is the answer to everything in life. When he prays throughout the day, he not only gives better care to his patients, but he is much more attentive to their families, as well. When he prays throughout the day he remembers to slow down, follow his intuition, and reach out for help when needed. Garret's comments are not unusual for people who have practiced the Eleventh Step of the twelve-step programs. I will offer some pointers on this later in the book.

I absolutely believe in the power of prayer. I have hundreds of stories about things happening to me or to others that are completely inexplicable otherwise. For example, at one point I decided to leave the addiction recovery field and go back into business to make some money. I convinced myself that it was the right thing to do (because I can sell myself anything). So my buddy got me a job as a high-tech headhunter and less than a year later I realized I had made a mistake. I quit that job and on an impulse, headed to Aspen for the weekend. I attended a twelve-step meeting there and afterward asked a guy to show me where the trailhead was for Conundrum in the Maroon Bells. I should have called it the Moron Bells because I should not have got on that trailhead by myself late at night with only a headlamp and no clue what I was doing. I was really running from myself.

After about five miles of hiking in the dark I ended up getting completely lost. I crossed a river a few times and I began stepping on parts of tree branches that had fallen, and they would break into pieces underneath my feet with every step. I became scared for my life because I had not told anyone where I was going. Eventually, I decided to stop and sleep underneath the stars and try to hike out in the morning.

The next morning I began my trek out of the mountains. I was full of fear from the night before and I prayed *for real*. I asked God where He wanted me and I sensed it was Estes Park—a thought that did not fill me with happiness. I felt embarrassed to go back to the place that I had left the year before to "conquer the business world." I had a lease in Denver, there were no real marriage prospects in that little retirement mountain town, and there were no good job prospects, either. Additionally, I was in debt from graduate school loans. There were no logical reasons why I should return to Estes, but I listened because I was rattled and because I was willing.

I found my way out of the forest and headed toward Estes. When I rolled into town I naturally returned to my old home group—a strange collection of mountain folk. I ran into Dan, with whom I'd played hoops from time to time, and discovered he was going through a tough time because his girlfriend (who would become his wife a few years later) had left town and stated that if he did not clean up his act it would be over between them. She'd taken a teaching position in a high school with a disadvantaged population of kids and had found her calling. It did not look like she was coming back.

At the time Dan was the manager of a small resort, and he offered to let me live with him in the manager quarters. He knew I was a counselor so he thought he would have a live-in hostage to prove to his girlfriend that he meant business this time. I accepted on the spot—free rent and a hot tub right outside my room! From those less-than-pure motives on both our parts nevertheless began of one of the greatest friendships I have ever known.

Within twenty-four hours of that encounter I ran into another old friend, Mary. She had been a private detective–turned–meth-smuggler from Arizona who had cleaned up her act and was presently working as a housekeeper for the rehabilitation center where I'd worked the previous year. She said, "We were talking about you yesterday because we thought you would be great for the new position that the center created." It was an afternoon-evening counselor position to do workshops and oversee the community after the staff went home at 5 p.m. It was perfect for me because I could cross-country ski or hike in Rocky Mountain National Park in the morning, go to a noon meeting, grab some lunch and head off to work during the week as well as have weekends free. It was perfect for a single guy who wanted to take advantage of what the mountains had to offer. Needless to say, I jumped at the job when it was offered.

Within a month of my return to the mountains my mother called and offered to pay off my student loans. She said that she and my father had invested in my brother-in-law's startup company. They hadn't expected to get any return, but the business had become a success, giving them enough of a return on their investment so that they could use it to help me.

A few years later it would be in that very town that I'd meet my wife. This process all started with a simple prayer and a willingness to follow the direction that I received. No valor—just a crazy dude and a sincere conversation with God.

Many times our prayers seem to go unanswered but it is important to persist in praying. We learn that praying for God's will, not our own, is the answer to most everything.

It is the daily conversation that we hold in our hearts throughout the day that will prove to be the most fulfilling relationship we can imagine. God resides in you. When you tap into that fact it will change your life, and the lives of others, for the better.

Service and Joy

When you gain the inner knowledge that you are secure, there will be a natural progression—you will realize that it is time to give freely from those things that have been freely given you. A sense of true purpose will develop and it will transmit hope to others. I'm not suggesting that you will become an evangelist. But I do believe that you will want to help those who want what they see in you. People will seek you out because they will want what you have. I am not referring to material possessions, but to the inner qualities of serenity and joy. You will experience an eagerness to help others "for free and for fun," because this is the life you will have come to love and cherish and your heart will hope that others receive this gift, too.

Paradoxically, when you help others by means of a life of service, you actually help yourself. This is simple, but it is not easy. The miracle is when you feel gratitude even for the problems that brought you to a way of life that gets better each day. There is an abundant amount of joy that comes from living a spiritual way of life.

A friend of mine said, "By living this way of life I get a daily reprieve from being anxious, angry, and uncomfortable." The same friend spoke about being of service and leaving the results up to God. He tries not to have an opinion as to where he thinks he "should be" spiritually, financially, and career- or otherwise. He realizes that he is exactly where he needs to be in order to grow up and fully experience life.

Mission

You have been created for a purpose, and you have unique gifts that only you can offer to others. Although you may not think so, it is likely that your worst experiences are also your greatest asset when it comes to helping others. When others who are also hurting see your healed or healing wounds, it inspires them to identify their own wounds and ask for help. Whatever you discover about yourself is what needs to be transmitted by your actions, as you begin living with clear mission and vision. I will show you how to craft a personal mission statement and start putting your hopes and dreams into action.

My Hope for You

My hope is that you give this way of living a chance. Most healthy and permanent change begins with some form of mental or emotional pain. I hope you are in enough pain to want to make the changes I suggest in this book, which are inspired by the Twelve Steps of addiction recovery. It is simple but, again, not easy. This way of life has worked, for me and for millions. I want to offer these tools of recovery and Christian values to you and to any person who wants help, healing, happiness, and purpose—whether or not they suffer from addiction. Apply the principles that are suggested here and complete the tasks. As we say in recovery, "Do not give up before the miracle!" The gift of fulfillment is the byproduct of this process.

CHAPTER TWO
The Truth

"Then you will know the truth and the truth will set you free."

—John 8:32

Moments of pure joy and a true sense of purpose are byproducts of a spiritual process that takes a serious commitment. The miracle begins when you stop fighting. It is time to stop using whatever weapons or defenses you typically use and try a different way that leads to positive change. A friend of mine described this process as painful and beautiful at the same time.

Think about the experience of being in the dark—let's say a dark movie theater—and then walking out into the daylight. It shocks your system—even causing pain—until your eyes adjust to the light. You blink and shade your eyes at first, and then you see that there is a real world outside to enjoy if you just hang in there until your vision adjusts. Eventually, reality becomes the thing you seek because it brings such rich rewards. How sad it would be if the sunlight of the real world was so painfully bright that you ran back inside the theater to take shelter in the fantasy world, in the darkness, instead of bracing yourself to face the light.

Essentials for the Work

Honesty with self, acceptance, open-mindedness, willingness, and eventually surrender are the internal qualities necessary for positive change and growth toward a life of true fulfillment. People seem to need a certain degree of pain and dissatisfaction with their current life condition or else the motivation will not be there for a meaningful and sustained commitment to the process.

Honesty or being true to oneself is the only place to start this inner journey. Sometimes the spiritual process begins with a crisis that may be as traumatic as a divorce or as subtle as being sick and tired of your situation. Occasionally, these events happen to us in a painful moment of clarity, like the realization that "She is not coming back—and my abusive words and actions helped drive her away," or "My inability to get past my resentments and pride contributed to his shutting down to me emotionally." Whatever the realization, there are usually different points throughout our lives when it is time to see the truth while we still have time to get off the downward-plummeting elevator.

What is it that bothers you? It will usually be something concerning a relationship, work, money, physical heath, psychological or emotional health, addiction, codependency, or spiritual crisis. In most cases, it will be a combination of factors leading to life becoming unmanageable. It is really hard to see, admit, and accept personal problems because the human ego is busy protecting us from looking too deeply into ourselves. We will see the problems and faults of others far more quickly than we see inside ourselves. The unhealthy part of ourselves sometimes creates apathy or shame, or keeps us in self-blinding pride. Either way, these qualities can keep us stuck for years, and sometimes decades. We need to get past the procrastination, self-justification, minimization, rationalization, guilt, and shame into a place of self-honesty and acceptance of reality.

In my work with addicts, it still amazes me how people can keep themselves in low levels of awareness about the reality of their condition. People sometimes judge themselves by their intentions while the world around them is judging them by their actions. We are usually the last people to realize the total truth about ourselves. Regardless, each person must come to his or her own inner honesty and truth, or the process of true transformation will be fleeting. I believe in intervention from external forces, but over time the motivation for change must move from external to internal or it will fade away.

To understand things from a heart level as opposed to a head level is a key to this part of the process. There are plenty of messed-up smart people who continue to make the same life mistakes over and over again. Intelligence can actually be an obstacle to receiving the help we need. It often takes high achievers even longer than ordinary people to see the unmanageability in their lives because their ego will hide behind their intelligence, accomplishments, and bank accounts. For example, sometimes it will take months of treatment or therapy before an intelligent person truly realizes how his or her reliance on intellect at the expense of emotional availability has caused a complete disconnect with his or her children.

I had the privilege of hiring a counselor named Michael who told a powerful story about how the spiritual process has unfolded in his life. He is a hardworking and straightforward guy with good insight and some insecurity. He is thirtysomething and single and is an excellent example of how the application of spiritual principles can transform pain and suffering into healing for self and others. Michael came from a broken home. His father is black and his mother is white, and he explained to me that he never felt as though he fit in anywhere. He had anger toward his dad for leaving when Michael needed him. Michael developed coping skills that were maladaptive, even though they helped him survive physically. Eventually they drove him into a world of dysfunction that—however it looked to others—seemed normal to him.

He eventually hit bottom and reached out for help. At the age of thirty he put himself into an eighteen-month behavior modification program.

Three weeks into the program he woke up looking out the window. He recalls, "I heard and felt the sun rising and I knew my old life was over." He experienced the beginning of a huge internal transformation. Fear left him that day and within a relatively short period of time, he became a leader in the institution into which he had placed himself.

Michael embraced the principles of twelve-step recovery and became part of a network of people with a common illness and a common solution. Today he works a strong program by continuing to grow spiritually every day. The application of spiritual concepts has led him to a life where fitness and nutrition have become important, as well as healthy relationships. Last year I listened to him give a talk to hospital personnel on cognitive behavioral therapy, and it was beautiful to see how he helps others because he was helped. He feels no self-pity and makes no excuses for his past life. He takes 100 percent responsibility for his own attitudes and circumstances. Something shifted inside of him when he got completely honest with himself and accepted his circumstances.

A friend I admire very much told me about his moment of truth, which he recalled with crystal-clear precision from twenty-six years prior. He had been married for over sixteen years and with his employer for fourteen years as a professor at a prestigious university. He had a fifteen-year-old son and three-year-old daughter. He had told his elderly parents that he would call them that evening to plan a visit. He started drinking with a friend at lunchtime and they did not quit until midnight, when they went to a diner for food and coffee.

As he recalls, it was 3:30 a.m. while driving home on the highway when he realized that he'd forgotten to call his parents or his wife. He realized that he was not being the father he wanted to be to his little girl and he admitted that his alcohol consumption was an issue, and that he was the problem. He decided that he needed help. When he got home he woke his wife and explained. She replied "good," rolled over angry, and went back to sleep.

The next day he called his insurance provider—they had him meet with an alcohol counselor the next day. She asked him a few questions, and then, based on his answers, she self-disclosed about her own alcoholism and recovery. She gave him a few suggestions but no mandates. He related to almost everything she shared with him.

That evening he took his wife and kids with him to his first twelve-step meeting, where there were about seven people who shared their stories very briefly. On the drive home, his wife, who had been telling him for years that he was an alcoholic, concluded that he did not qualify. He had not lost his job, family, health, or money like the people in the meeting. My friend told his wife that he was indeed an alcoholic and that he belonged with that group of people. His life began with the moment of truth on a highway at 3:30 a.m. when he accepted the fact that he could not help himself and that he would need to reach out for help from others.

Many moments of truth are characterized by the dropping of blame and self-pity, which results in embracing the responsibility to change. These realizations can happen at any stage of our spiritual development. Sometimes the very things that sustained you at an earlier time in life can become the things you need to change. I have a buddy named John, who from the outside appears to have it all. He is athletic and successful as a top sales manager for a large sporting goods company, has healthy kids and a supportive wife. He has plenty of money, is well connected to his church, is a very talented musician, and he is in solid recovery from the illness of addiction. At the time of this story, he was mentoring several men and he was highly regarded in the twelve-step recovery world. John was known as a hard-ass recovering twelve-step fundamentalist who did not care what his sponsees were feeling; he had been taught by his sponsors that the program was all about action and results. He had a strong belief in his God and a strong belief that he knew how a twelve-step program should be worked.

Then he moved to another state for his job. He tried to connect to his old friendships but somehow it was not the same. He suffered a setback in his recovery and he needed to get honest with himself and make some big changes. He changed his sponsor, his church, and the meetings that he was attending. He began therapy for the trauma he'd experienced throughout his youth, and he started to get in touch with his emotions. John's old sponsors had not asked nor seemed to care about his feelings, but his new sponsor was constantly asking him how he felt. John is now becoming a lighthearted, tender man who still commands huge respect from others. He was honest enough with himself to admit and accept that it was time to change his belief system even though that belief system had kept him abstinent from his addictions for years. He has serious courage.

John told me that "I listen more these days and I do not try to impose my beliefs onto others anymore." He stated that he has become more accepting, tolerant, and compassionate with himself and others. He continues to hold his core beliefs about God but he explained that the same men whom he had judged in his past have become friends and teachers to him in his new group. He stated, "I do not want false identities; I want to do whatever it takes to heal and find my true self." He finished by stating that "I am who I am and I am God's child, and I want to derive my worth and satisfaction from that fact."

Paul grew up in a broken home and lacked enduring connections. He was passed around to several family members throughout his childhood. He is a handsome guy with many talents, but he suffered from PTSD, addiction, and lots of anger and lust. After a long series of misfortunes such as losing his baseball scholarship because of his attitude, he was living in Breckenridge, Colorado, and working as a snowboard instructor. One night he got drunk and was arrested. As he was being processed into the local jail, he experienced a moment of clarity and realized that he *did this all to himself*. There was no one to blame for his life anymore—people like his alcoholic/abusive father were long gone. He saw himself in the reflection of the glass and felt the gift of desperation. He admitted the truth that he could not fix himself (successfully stop drinking, change himself, and be happy). He reached out for help. His mother offered to bail him out but he rejected her offer because he did not trust himself to be free—he knew he would drink. She helped him secure a lawyer and coincidentally, his lawyer understood addiction and referred him to a treatment center—and his life of healing began. It all started with the painful admission of the truth about himself. He was given a moment of grace. Paul's problem manifested in addiction, but there are thousands of variations to his story. His profound moment of deep pain and truth in the mountain town jail cell was the foundation for his spiritual experience, which would lead to a life of fulfillment.

Some of us need to experience how messed up we are without God's help and guidance before we are ready for change. In twelve-step recovery, they say that you have to concede to your innermost self that you are addicted. A deep level of honesty and acceptance can lead you to see how powerless you are over certain aspects of your life. In some sense we are all addicts. Your thing might not be a chemical, but you have your own version of drugs. They may come in the form of entertainment, money, fitness, power, prestige, being needed, being liked and respected, being loved and accepted, food, anger, pornography, physical appearance, popularity, career and work, religion—or anything else that has more power over you than you have over it. Again, what is your problem, obsession, or addiction? You would not be human if you did not have problems or challenges. What is it in your case? (As you answer, try to avoid the thinking that the cause of your problems lies outside of yourself.)

I have hit several bottoms in my life—some were false bottoms and some were authentic. My first one, described above in detail while driving in the Jeep, started with psychic pain and ended with a peace that I had never felt before or after to that extent. Many people think they have hit a bottom only to realize in hindsight that it was a false bottom. As a rule, any time your bottom has a solution that you can effect all by yourself, it will turn out to be a "false bottom" because your ego (Edging God Out) is still "large and in charge."

But if you are reading this book you must be looking for some sort of answer. A well-known Jesuit speaker used to tell a story about a person for whom existence was like living in a sewer. If someone offered to help get him out, he'd answer something like, "No, no, I'm fine. But could you guys stop making waves? I keep having to swallow all this crap."

People in trouble may say things like, "Give me my reputation back or give me my wife back." Maybe they will say, "Help me get my money back or help me get people off my back." There are many variations, but the concept is simple: "I think I know what is best for me." Most people do not want the true solution; instead, they just want to get their way and for *you* to stop making waves.

You will not be able to move forward until you come to a place of acceptance with yourself or your situation. It seems like a paradox that if you want to experience true change you need to first and foremost accept everything the way it currently is. How does that work? Coming to a place of acceptance is similar to admitting truth, which propels us into reality. We do not need to like it but we do need to accept it because it is what it is. The less we accept, the more we fight with, run from, avoid, or try to manipulate life. Honesty coupled with acceptance is a powerful combination that ignites the internal change process.

You cannot receive the gift of a healthy spiritual life that leads to fulfillment until you look within and get honest from your heart. What is it that you need to get honest about? What do you need to accept about your circumstances? What are the facts about your current condition? What are you using to fill the void?

The task for this chapter is to journal about your issues:
- Review and comment on the questions in Chapter One. For example, what do you believe are your problems?
- Write about the ways in which you have tried to control your issue or problem—such as your debt, anger, relationship, eating, etc.
- For each of these, what were the outcomes?
- What are the negative consequences in each case? For example, "By working eighty-hour weeks, I've become very distant from my wife and now she wants a divorce."
- How do you feel as you get these things down on paper? Make sure that you attach a feeling word (angry, sad, hurt, happy, etc.) after each negative consequence.
- Are you ready to get help? What are you willing to do?
- Are you open to utilizing practical spiritual concepts even if they may not seem to directly address your issues?

Once we establish a certain degree of self-honesty, it leads us to the next task or phase of development. When we get honest with ourselves, it is time to get out of the problem and into the solution—immediately. You have no time to waste!

The gift of getting something from the head to the heart is a true miracle and is worth more than money can buy. When you realize how powerless you are over people, places, and things, it marks the beginning of a profound spiritual experience. There are aspects of ourselves that cannot be conquered by determination, intellect, or willpower. Someone may think, "I made it through law school with a full-time job so I know I can do anything if I put my mind to it." It may be true that you have accomplished the almost impossible, but there are some things, like addiction, that cannot be conquered by willpower alone. When you catch a cold, all the willpower in the world won't help you stop your nose from running. When it comes to certain aspects of life, we need to give up rather than fight on. I am not going to ask you to fight harder. I am going to suggest that you stop overusing your willpower and let yourself open up to the real power.

CHAPTER THREE

Is There Hope for Us?

"No man is excluded from calling upon God, the gate of salvation is set open unto all men: neither is there any other thing which keepeth us back from entering in, save only our own unbelief."

—John Calvin

We need something bigger than ourselves to believe in and we need to acquire faith, which produces the courage we need to face life's challenges. We will be missing out on the best life has to offer if we do not tap into the spirit that dwells within us.

If you have identified some of your problems and issues with honesty and accepted your circumstances without blaming the world around you, then you are ready to proceed with our work. In contemporary society we seem open-minded about technology, but increasingly closed-minded about spirituality. There are many reasons for this, including prejudice against certain religious fanatics that have lead people astray, negative past experiences, or our insistence on empirical evidence.

The core of your current task is to stay open-minded, especially if you have been on some either specifically religious or specifically secular path. When we are open-minded we are reachable and teachable. The question is pretty simple, "Are you willing to believe in the possibility of a Higher Power? Are you willing to believe that God (Higher Power, Creator, Spirit of the Universe) could help you with your problems and issues?" If you have a belief in God, then the question is, "Are you willing to have God or a Higher Power reveal Him- or Itself to you in a different way?" For example, if you are a Christian and believe in your heart that Jesus is the only way to the Father, I am not asking you to challenge or let go of that belief, but I am asking you to allow Jesus to meet you in an entirely different way. Christ encountered the most difficulty with religious people because they tended to be convinced that they knew what or who God was supposed to be based on the scriptures. On the other hand, individuals who felt they were hopeless—tax collectors, prostitutes, and uneducated fisherman—could see what the teachers of the scriptures could not. Would you walk past Jesus if he were here today because of your current perceptions and belief system?

In the rooms of recovery you will hear people say, "We came, we came to, we came to believe." Coming to believe is a process that goes deeper and deeper every year that you commit yourself to the work. One thing is for sure: there is a lot more going on than you can see around you. Science can easily prove that fact. We are typically open to trying many things, such as medication or alcohol, yoga or exercise, new employment or a new marriage, and so on. What about being open to prayer—even if you do not yet believe in anything? How could that hurt?

Could it hurt to try praying for help with your decisions before you actually change careers? If you have a serious problem such as an addiction, depression, or anxiety, then would you consider praying and asking this Power to help bring you to a place of peace and happiness? I ask these questions because I frequently counsel intelligent people like yourself, who would rather experiment with potentially life-threatening drugs in their search to feel whole than consider seeking a relationship with God or a Higher Power.

Before moving forward, you need to get clear about the thoughts and actions that have consistently not worked for you. What do you keep doing over and over again while expecting a different result? Take, for instance, the person who thinks their place of employment is completely screwed up (which—by the way—it probably is). Let me describe something to you that is even more screwed up: thinking that by going "over there" (meaning the next place of employment), things will be different, better, and you will be happier, etc. Nine times out of ten what you'll find is that "wherever you go, there you are." We tend to find what we are looking for, so eventually you will see all the dysfunction in your new place of employment, too. Just give it some time. The same goes for "serial monogamists." Unhappy with their partner, they divorce and seek happiness with someone new—only to find they have married the "same person with a different face." What is the common denominator in these unhappy situations? Is it you?

What are the thoughts and actions that lead you back into a negative situation and thus to an undesirable outcome? Usually they include the idea that "this time, it's going to be different."

It is time now to begin shifting your paradigm. Wherever you are on the spiritual path, there is always room to grow and change. We will start by practicing simple suggestions like, "Do the next right thing," and "Bring the body and the mind will follow."

Many recovering people say the same thing in different words and expressions about this spiritual process. The beginning of the journey is not comfortable and sometimes very scary, but we take certain risks in order to try to overcome our situations (whatever they may be). When we begin to practice these simple, but not easy, tasks a new inner world opens up. We gain a new perspective and closeness with God that we did not think possible. We understand life from a different dimension that cannot be explained in words until you experience it. Life will still have its problems, but we have a drastically altered attitude toward the challenges. There are countless ways in which people come to realize that God or a Higher Power is real and that He, She, or It wants to be in a relationship with us.

I asked a friend of mine about how he came to believe in God, and he told me that his mentor had initially asked him to write about the attributes that he wanted his God to have. For instance, he wanted to know that God loved all people and that He would always be forgiving. He thought, "God, I need you not to criticize me when I screw up." He described how he still struggles with his understanding of God. However, he has some peace and knows that he does not need to have this figured out all at once. At first he thought he needed to do this "acquisition of faith thing" perfectly. He now believes that he has chosen a harder path by struggling so much and by testing and questioning everything. But that is his path and he can't imagine doing it any other way.

Even though he struggles with his beliefs, his relationship with his God, whom he does not yet understand, is the most important thing in his life. His God comes to him through friends, through love of his wife, through prayer and meditation, and the people whom he helps. It comes through spiritual readings and his art as well as the teachings and fellowship he has with his church. It is evident that there is a power manifesting itself in his life because he does not act out addictively anymore, and even when he struggles, he is able to get back to right thinking instead of self-destructing.

I have been really lucky over the past seven years to work closely with a clinician named Gustavo. He grew up in a first-generation immigrant Mexican family. He became a street kid and experienced many problems until he surrendered and admitted himself to a long-term substance abuse program.

Since I've known him, Gustavo has graduated from college, received a master's degree, gone through divorce, opened his own recovery home, wrote and published a book on Dialectal Behavioral Therapy and the Twelve Steps, and became the Team Leader for the University of Colorado CeDAR men's program. He is also a poet, plays music, and has participated in demonstrations for social justice. He has half custody of his three beautiful daughters, whom he loves very much. He remains dedicated to twelve-step recovery and, no matter how busy his life gets, he always makes it to his meetings and makes time for his work with his sponsor.

Gustavo never had positive mentors or spirituality in his life until about ten years ago. He always had a sense of feeling lost and yearning for some sort of connection. He told me that when he was thirteen he crossed the border into Juarez, Mexico, where a woman started talking to him about Jesus. He remembered wanting the peace that he saw in her eyes.

Later in life when Gustavo entered recovery and picked his sponsor, LJ, he did so because he was attracted to LJ's sense of peace, and the fact that he spoke about spiritual concepts. He said, "If I didn't tap into this spiritual stuff, I was screwed." LJ "talked the talk and walked the walk." Over many months and years he developed trust in LJ to the point that he trusted him with his life. In Gustavo's words, "To hope and to trust are the most important things we do."

As Gustavo and I talked he kept saying, "If you want to talk about spirituality you need to speak with my sponsor." (Gustavo is very spiritual himself, but it is typical of a truly spiritual person to see those qualities in others before seeing them in themselves.) Gustavo attends his meetings in the inner city; he believes people there are "real," and he loves them. He feels their pain and he wants to give back to those he considers "his people." In these twelve-step meetings he feels the power of God through shared pain, growth, and victory over huge obstacles.

In my own life, this process of "coming to believe" in the love and power of God has evolved throughout the twenty-two years that I have been seeking. It is a process, not an event, even though I point to many events as examples. One episode in my process began shortly after my 1991 conversion experience.

In a Boston bar I used to frequent, I had won an all-expenses-paid trip to Cancun. But then I entered recovery, and asking the drinking buddy I'd planned to invite on the trip didn't seem like such a good idea anymore.

I asked my dad to join me instead, because I thought he'd be a safe companion for me and that we could connect a little during the trip.

He agreed to accompany me, and so there I was in Mexico with my dad. I was a few months sober and emotionally unstable. I asked him if he believed in God and if so, why—not something very common for Irish New York Catholics like us to sit around and have a chat about. He told me a few cool stories. He told me that at a very young age he had figured out what he thought was a neat way to park his parents' car given their narrow driveway in Bay Ridge, Brooklyn. My dad would back it out across the street and into the neighbors' driveway on the other side of the road. Then he'd put it into drive and gun it back across the street into his parents' garage. One day, as he paused the car in the neighbor's driveway, he threw it into drive and nothing happened. The engine turned off and the car didn't move, which had never happened before. At that instant, out on the cross street, a car barreled past. My dad is sure that he would have been killed if his parents' car hadn't stalled. He is convinced that God intervened.

He and I had a decent week, but he had to leave a couple of days before me, so there I was in Cancun: solo, dry, and crazy. I met some women and they invited me on a booze cruise. Of course I accepted. The first thing that happened is that one of the cruise workers tried to pour a shot of tequila into my mouth as I boarded the vessel. Since he didn't speak English, I told him that I was allergic to alcohol and that I would "break out in handcuffs" from it (a common expression in the rooms of recovery). Needless to say, within five minutes I found myself with a drink in each hand, thinking that no one would know if I drank, that I could start (recovery) over once I got back to the U.S. These thoughts scared me, so I began to pray. "God, I need intervention right now because I am going down!" Within seconds, I heard myself blurting out to the woman sitting next to me: "I'm trying to lose weight and I promised myself I wouldn't drink." Fortunately, she was quite supportive of my decision and took both drinks out of my hands. I walked to the side of the boat, looked up at the stars, and thought about how close I had come to taking that drink. In hindsight, I believe it was a "God shot" because I asked for help, and I received it. I've had enough experiences like this to know that if I *sincerely* want God in my life, He will show up.

God will show up in as many different ways as there are people. All we need is to attempt to cultivate the values of honesty, open-mindedness, and willingness. Many people arrive on the spiritual path based on a series of what seem to be inexplicable coincidences. I remember sitting in a twelve-step recovery meeting in Boston during a visit to my parents and listening to a gruff, older Irish guy speak. He said that he had not been able to sleep the night before, so he had decided to read. As he finished the book, which was called *Ninety Minutes in Heaven,* he looked at the clock—it was the exact time and date of his son's death a year prior. This gave him consolation that his son and God were letting him know that "all was well."

If you struggle with the whole "God idea" like many of us do, it may be helpful to look back on the coincidences in your life. Look at the random events that have unfolded and look for your God in each. Who were the people or things placed before you at certain times throughout the seasons of your life? Maybe you were introduced to a particular sport or a form of artistic expression at just the right time. Maybe someone introduced you to the world of science, the written word, or a youth group. Maybe someone believed in you when you did not believe in yourself. What we don't want to do is confuse God with religion—they are very different things. Religion can help point you toward your God, like a map can help you see your desired destination, but you can never confuse the map of a place with the actual place itself.

There are many people who have strayed from their faith because they feel like they have tried the whole "God thing" or "religious deal" and it did not "work out." Sometimes people look at the world and their lives and think, "If there was a God, why did He do this? Or why did He not do that?" I'm reminded of a cathartic release I felt during therapy once. By using guided imagery I was brought back to an experience in my youth at a time when I thought exactly this way ("Why does God do this and not that?"). During that experience I was surrounded by a bunch of teenagers and was about to fight someone a lot bigger and meaner than me. I was scared of what was about to happen and felt upset that the other kids would actually participate in this event by watching or egging it on. I was hurt and angry that there was no one there to protect me or stick up for me. I felt so alone. I felt abandoned by God. As my pain and tears started to flow, I began to understand that God was always with me throughout my entire life—especially in the pain. Something happened to me when I realized that God *was* there with me in my distress. It gave me the courage to go back and experience the necessary discomfort to heal from many of these events.

I have experienced hundreds, if not thousands, of moments where I received hope by opening myself up to my Creator. When I look back over the past two decades since I consciously began walking on a spiritual path, I realize that most of the profound things that happened to me I only understood through later reflection.

I had some very distorted perceptions of God. Over time, I believe God has been healing my toxic images of Him so I can grow in intimacy with Him and His children. I use certain words for God, but you are obviously free to use whatever words you choose to identify and describe your Higher Power. There is lots of wisdom in the invitation to develop your own conception of God, because we have many—often unhelpful—images associated with certain words and concepts. Some of these images are toxic, so we want to make the point of entry as broad as possible—excluding no one. One of the biggest contributions of the twelve-step approach is the notion of God-as-you-understand-Him or Her. Or even, It.

We want to gain clarity about whatever toxic ideas we hold, because our distortions can keep us from availing ourselves of the most important dimension of our lives—conscious union with our Creator. Every November for several years, I would cofacilitate a generic twelve-step retreat with a friend of mine, Fr. Dick Dunphey, S.J., at the Sacred Heart Retreat House in Sedalia, Colorado. Sadly, Dick passed on during the writing of this book, and I will miss not only his friendship but the ability to present this material with him. Dick had some interesting thoughts on our common toxic misunderstandings of God, which I will paraphrase here.

First, there is the distant and uninvolved God who watches from the heavens but is not interested in our day-to-day struggles. We think things like, "If God cared about this world so much, then why does God let _____ happen?" Even though many Americans believe in God, a good portion does not believe that He cares about the intimate details of their lives. Many people would even go as far as to judge people as naive who believe in a God who cares about them. Even people who consider themselves spiritual often perceive individuals who pursue a personal relationship with God as unenlightened. My friend talks about a distant God as the opposite of what the Old and New Testaments describe. God is constantly trying to be in a relationship with us, but we need to reciprocate. I like the saying, "If you do not feel close to God, then ask yourself—who moved?"

Another popular misunderstanding of God is that God is an authoritarian or critical parent. This is the God I described earlier, the one who is going to get fed up with us and come down on us with fury. At the very least we are going to be punished for our sins and failures and God is disappointed in us. Instead of looking at our sins (missing the mark of perfection) as the punishment in itself, we believe we will be punished for our failures. This creates a sense of shame that keeps us from wanting to seek God as the solution to our lives. We superimpose our judgmental and condemning attitudes onto this all all-forgiving Source of Life.

Early in my spiritual journey it would take me days and sometimes weeks to get back to God after a period of separation. I felt so much shame about myself that I did not want to talk to Him again about the same mistakes I had made a thousand times. Now I look at how quickly I can get back to God with an open heart as indicative of my spiritual health. The more I experience God's grace, forgiveness, and power, the less I feel as though He is going to eventually get sick of me. An old friend of mine once said, "It is God's job to love me, but now I know that He actually likes me."

A couple of years ago my friend and pastor asked me to share some of my experiences as a member of the church at a service and I agreed. The night before I was to speak I'd had a fight with my wife and in the morning I felt emotionally hung-over, so I texted him and said I did not want to share my experience because I felt like a fraud. He told me to get my butt to church and get over myself. After I shared, I saw how much God had worked in my life over the two years we had been attending, and I was able to get back on track.

There are many ways to move past the lie that God is counting our sins and waiting for us to mess up. People who really care for you can help you when you are stuck with the critical parent or God in your psyche. Usually a good friend, mentor, or nurturing family member has a better perspective of us than we have of ourselves. God can work through these individuals to show us the truth about God's love for us.

Then there is the God of conditional love. Here the prevailing idea is that we need to make ourselves worthy of His love. I used to think that if I stayed out of trouble and was a good boy then God would be pleased with me and hear and answer my prayers. After years of falling way short (in my mind), I slowly adopted an attitude that said, "I am going to hell, but at least I'm enjoying myself." But in truth I wasn't enjoying myself at all, because I was consciously disconnected from the Source of my life. I left the God who dwells within me for the distant land of a false self.

My life completely changed for the better when I realized that I could not ever become who I thought I needed to be. I did not have the necessary power. I kept thinking, *If I just put my mind to it I can do it better this time.* It was actually the opposite. I admitted that I could not become the man that I wanted to be with my own resources and that I wanted and needed God's help. Then I experienced a feeling of love and total acceptance from God—something I will never be able to adequately describe. We are accepted and loved for exactly who we are right now. That does not mean that God leaves us this way. It appears as though God wants to help us in our quest for self-improvement when He is actually invited into the process without conditions.

My friend talks about another toxic image that suggests that God could never love a person like me. The underlying thought is that "I am defective." This is a form of false humility and needs to be overcome by good therapy and a strong spiritual community. The truth is that "God does not make junk." Everyone has his or her strengths and liabilities. Sometimes it is our character flaws that—once surrendered and redeemed—become our greatest gift to those around us. It is important to talk with God about God's thoughts and feelings about us. Go right to the source and ask with a gentle and open heart.

For this chapter, your task is to consider and then write down your answers to the following questions.

- What would you want God to be to you if you could ask for any type of relationship?
- What are your toxic images of God? Or what have been your distorted images of a Higher Power?
- What have been your negative experiences with religion?
- Where do your religious beliefs come from? Are you willing to examine those beliefs?
- How do you view nature? And the feeling, act, or concept of love?
- Do you believe there is hope for you? If yes, why? If no, why not?
- Are you willing to give the idea of an "all-loving God" a chance?

My job is not to judge, but to discern what is good and true. As the bumper sticker saying goes, "Blessed are the flexible, for they shall not be bent out of shape."

There are millions of people who will never experience the gift of true spiritual belief as a result of their intellectualism and need for hard facts, as well as negative past experiences, fear of looking like a religious weirdo, false gods like material success, and overall fear-based self-reliance. I would venture to say that most people will not earnestly seek God based upon fear alone. Fear of what others will think, fear that the fun will be over, fear of becoming "lame," fear of the unknown, fear of change, fear that they will not find anything and be more disillusioned, fear of being like the people in those "spiritual" TV shows that frighten you when you think that there are people who will buy the crap that some of these people are selling.

You are (hopefully) seeking the opposite of fear, which is faith. You will need to define what that looks like for you. I would suggest that you could ask God or your Higher Power for help with this process. The process of attaining belief or faith is a lifelong deal, and you can be happy that you are on the field, playing, versus in the parking lot, drinking and missing out on life.

It starts with the question, "What can you believe right now?" and "What do you believe?" It is time to decide to surrender to, and to rely on, something greater than yourself (the God of your understanding). Getting those thoughts down on paper and sharing them with somebody is important. In the end, our understanding has to be something that we come to on our own terms.

My friend ended his discussion about toxic images with these thoughts on the tragic and terrible events that took place on September 11, 2001. Due to modern communications technology, we are privileged to know what thousands of people think and do when they know they are about to die. Do they cry out to God for revenge? No—in the face of certain death, what they thought of was life; and they thought of those they loved. What did these people do when they knew they were going to die? They told somebody else how much they loved them.

Mark Bingham calls his mother to tell her that he loves her. Todd Beemer calls an operator to ask her to call his wife to tell her how much he loves her. Jeremy Glick tells his wife, "I love you. Be brave." Veronique Bowen phones her mom, "There is smoke everywhere; I think I'm trapped. I love you." And Jason Johnson calms his wife, "If you tell me that you love me, it will be alright."

These were ordinary people, not saints, but they did not bemoan their fates or cry out in fear. They called out to those they were leaving behind, in love. They tried to make their own imminent deaths easier for their loved ones to bear. They expressed the true nature, and not the toxic notion, of God: love.

CHAPTER FOUR

Willingness to Surrender—Let Go and Let God

"Be not angry that you cannot make others as you wish them to be, since you cannot make yourself as you wish to be."

—Thomas á Kempis, *Imitation of Christ*

So what is the real problem with us humans? We in the recovery world have made the discovery that we are all manipulators to one degree or another, although our manipulations are sometimes very difficult to ascertain. There are thousands of forms of manipulation, but most of them have at their root the need to maintain some sort of dependence upon or domination of others (we are usually quite unaware of these destructive traits). We rationalize: "But I am just trying to help! People need to act right! This world needs to change!" The problem with that approach is that it's like seeking medical treatment for a rash and having the doctor say, "Here, take this cream and apply it to the skin of everyone around you (your wife, husband, boss, the IRS, etc.) and you will immediately start to feel better!" Put this way, you can easily see how silly we are when we try to change others in order to make ourselves feel better. But that's what most of our manipulations are usually attempting to do.

If the cause of my emotions and the basis of my self-worth lie outside of myself, then of course I need to constantly manipulate others to get them to do what I want (to love me, accept me, admire me, buy this product from me, take care of me, let me take care of them, etc.). These habits are embedded in the fabric of who we become over time so we do not even know it is a problem. It *is* a problem because it does not work. It gets worse even if we do get our way in life. If I get you to love me, or I get rich, or whatever else I manipulated my way into, now I have to keep it that way, and that brings fear of loss. Fearful thinking leads to fear-based action, which leads to unhappiness.

In the first thirty days of treatment at my hospital we only permit the clients one five-minute phone call per night. We impose this limit because we know that it is almost impossible to effectively manipulate people in less than five minutes. Now, give an addict three hours of face-to-face time on Sunday afternoon during family visitation and they will have those visitors right where they *think* they want them. Addicts are fearful of not getting their way. They want to be in control of others and they sure do not want anyone trying to control them. Addicts are extreme individuals but not very different from you.

What are the thoughts that occupy us? "What is going to make me secure and successful? What do I want? What are my needs?" These types of conscious and unconscious thoughts can guide our lives. Do you see then how we all become self-consumed in trying to get what we want or think we need?

Where Is Your Reliance?

Some people's control tactics are obvious while others are very subtle—so subtle that others do not even know that there is a hook on the end of their line. Some people can manipulate others by being kind and thoughtful. Can't someone just be a thoughtful and kind person? Absolutely. Many people are. But when manipulators are kind, it's with an ulterior motive, and unlike genuinely thoughtful persons, the manipulators become angry when their kindness doesn't have the intended result. Think of the manipulator who holds a door open for others and becomes angry when he or she doesn't get a "thank you" in return. The authentically kind person is rewarded with the knowledge that he or she helped another. The manipulator wants his or her "thank you."

We may manipulate others with our feelings, facial expressions, with what we say, what we do not say, and the list goes on. We can be intimidating or act helpless but what it boils down to is control. We try to control others because we do not trust that God is all we need. We trust in our thinking and not in God's Grace.

I heard a story about a health professional in Colorado who over the course of one year lost his business, his reputation, his wife, and custody of his children. He lost everything as a result of his addiction, including his savings, which he spent on lawyers and treatment. As he began the spiritual process of healing he knew he needed to surrender his life over to a loving God because he had done a lousy job of managing things his way. At one point he said, "I didn't realize that all I ever needed was God until God was all I had."

We seem to fight against the very aspect of our lives that can bring us the greatest amount of joy, freedom, purpose, and connection. We would rather try to become our own gods and create our own security. We want to achieve so that we can make ourselves relevant in a society that judges us on our profession, our house, our car, our body/looks, our education, our friends, and our bank account. We fearfully attempt to calculate how we can send our kids to the best colleges and still retire with the maximum level of comfort.

Many of us can't imagine following our dreams because they are not "practical." As a result of the denial of our dreams, we end up needing to live lives that give us security. When I lived in Guatemala, I was struck by the level of sincere gratitude and happiness in the midst of poverty. Many of the people I met were taking the verse "Give us this day our daily bread" very seriously. They were depending on God to provide for them for real. I am certainly not an advocate for poverty, but I do advocate placing our dependence on God.

Mother Theresa would talk about poverty in the West being so tragic because there is so much loneliness and emptiness and so many people who feel unloved or unwanted. They do not know how to see beyond material resources when what they're really missing is a living relationship with God. Again, there is nothing wrong with the material world if we see it in the right perspective, with our hearts and minds. Our reliance must be on the Creator of all—not on a job, on a person, on money, etc.

There is a biblical story that illustrates the crucial task of total surrender. A rich young man comes to Jesus and asks what he needs to do to obtain eternal life, and Jesus tells him to sell all his possessions, give his money to the poor, and follow Him. The young man walks away sad because he knows he can't give up his material wealth. This parable shows that there are so many things holding us back from truly "going the distance." When we surrender, ask for help, and give our life to God (whom neither you nor I will ever fully comprehend) it is a defining moment of our existence. I am reminded that when we contemplate surrender, our ego (Edging God Out) makes us feel as though our lives are over, but those of us who are aware of God's grace know that our lives have just begun.

We need to be willing to do anything necessary to be free from the cage of our selves. This does not mean that you will need to move to Africa and become a relief worker—it just means that you need to be *willing* to do so. Once the willingness is there, things seem to get so much easier.

Let Go and Let God

In order to attain real transformation and true results, you need to be willing to let go of control, and surrender. One definition of surrender is "to go over to the winning side." In the recovery world we say "surrender to win." It is a paradox.

There is a spark of the Divine within each of us, and it is our job to let go of whatever is blocking our access to it. The reason you do not feel totally satisfied is because your heart and soul yearn for a deep connection with the Divine. It is the God hunger that gets so obscured and pushed down that it does not even appear to exist. In recovery meetings you will hear people say that "You only need to know two things about God, 1) there is one and 2) you are not it!"

We can come to know this Creator in a way that enables us to go to Him with our wounds, with our sorrows, with our joys, with our questions, our hopes, our dreams, and with our relationships. This relationship—the one we have with the God of our understanding—has got to become paramount in our lives. If this relationship is not more important to us than our marriages or our children, we will try to play god ourselves.

Take the example of wanting the best for your children. I think any parent does, to a certain degree, worrying about them and trying hard to provide "the best" of everything. If you are placing your reliance on yourself to figure things out and to nurture them perfectly, you are probably worrying all the time, and will constantly be controlling because so much is riding on you. But if your reliance is on God, then you know that the power lies with Him and that you are the lucky individual who gets to care for His kids. The direction and the results are in His hands now, not yours. This frees you to love more fully and to accept those closest to you as God made them, as they really are.

When the computer company I was working for transferred me to Denver in early 1992, I didn't know what I wanted to do with my life. I had zero interest in computer hardware. I got depressed. I kept swearing off things like nicotine and women, telling myself that things were going to be different this time. I made strong efforts, but I would always slip back into old behaviors.

I drove to the mountains and decided that I was going to give my life over to my Creator and I was envisioning a "mountaintop experience." I was thinking that when I got to my destination I would throw my hands up and say a prayer, hoping an eagle would fly by or the clouds would part and the sun would shine down on me. I would know that my connection was made with my God. I was looking for a sign that said, "You're going to be okay, everything is going to be okay, my hand is upon you."

What actually happened was that my car bottomed out on the snow going up the mountain. I had to leave it behind and trudge up the hill to the top on foot. I got up there and I threw my hands up and I said a twelve-step recovery prayer: "God, I offer myself to Thee, to build with me and to do with me as Thou wilt. Relieve me of the bondage of self that I may better do Thy will. Take away my difficulties that victory over them may bear witness to those I would help, with Thy power, Thy love and Thy way of life that I may do Thy will always."

Silence. Nothing happened. No light, no birds, no eagle, no song, no peace, just a little wind in the face. So I walked back down to the car, which I couldn't get out of the snow, and I slammed my fist on the hood. I started screaming at God, raising my fist, saying, "What's wrong with you? Why can't you help me?" It was very dramatic, like a scene from a Hollywood movie.

Then the thought occurred to me that this behavior did not resemble that of someone who had just given his whole life and will over to the care of God, as he understood God. It didn't resemble that of someone who had even remotely surrendered. I asked myself, "What would it look like if I had truly surrendered?" If I had actually surrendered at the top of this mountain, I would be going to ask for help. I would be asking for help from somebody or something. So there I was, a transplanted New Yorker with a warped perception of people who lived in the mountains. I thought that they would be like hillbillies from central casting. I could almost hear the banjos. I could imagine some guy with his eye on me at that moment, ready to come after me if I trespassed. But I gathered my courage and I walked down the road about half a mile onto a marked property and knocked on the door. A man answered the door and said, "Can I help you?"

I said, "I don't know, maybe I can use your phone? I'm having car trouble."

He says, "Yeah, go ahead. It's a party line so if you hear someone, just hang up."

I didn't even know who I was going to call. It's not like I had AAA or anything. My mind was reeling, thinking, *Who should I call? What I am going to do?*

I was still undecided when behind me a hinge squealed, a floorboard squeaked, I wheeled around, and in walked. . . Dave. Dave and I had met at a Super Bowl party. He looked at me and said, "Mike, what are you doing in my brother's cabin?" I said, "I really don't know." Dave ended up taking me back up the mountain and helping me with the car. I ended up helping him and his brother install a wood stove. That evening Dave and I went down to Idaho Springs for a twelve-step meeting, and then out to dinner.

At dinner, Dave said, "I can't tell you, every time I am with my brother the last few years, we've fought. Since you were there, it really went a lot more smoothly than it ever has in recent years."

It dawned on me that I might never get that burning-bush, mountaintop, spiritual lollapalooza of an experience. I was not a medicine man for the Lakota. I was just a guy who was going to need to hang out with other guys who struggle and get through life together. And my God was going to send me people and send me books and send me situations. It was my job to open my eyes to these experiences and to know that help was on the way. It just was not going to come in the package that I had thought it would come in.

Usually, the process of surrender takes the form of listening and following the direction of another human being, like Bob. Bob was a guy I counseled in treatment years ago. He is a great guy—very personable. He used compulsive binge eating as a coping skill early in life to deal with uncomfortable emotions, and as he grew into adulthood, the behavior persisted and took its toll on his self-esteem. He also drank heavily. At the time we worked together, he had just graduated college and was working for a bank. He is one of those guys who are successful at anything they put their minds to even though they are tortured by their obsessions and wounds. He just started playing rugby in college and quickly became an amazing college player, able to travel and play throughout the States.

Bob said he was willing to go to any length to get free, but he struggled. I suggested that he go up to the mountains, to a lodge with a program that combines the spiritual and the physical to get people back on their feet. It's a long-term program, which takes a financial and time investment— an indication of someone's willingness to surrender to do whatever it takes to get his or her life on the right foundation. He went up there and had some struggles and bounced around a bit, but eventually he got on his feet. When looking for employment he humbled himself (a former banker) and took a low-level position at a golf course. He was able to play a lot of free golf and eventually became a golf pro, which enabled him to teach golf at a country club while he worked his spiritual program and took direction from his mentor.

After building a strong foundation applying these spiritual principles, he met the woman who would become his wife. He is currently finishing his master's degree in counseling while mentoring other guys and moving forward. He is part owner of a business in which he helps newly recovering men address their life issues. Although his life isn't perfect (and whose is?) he is finding success—by working and following direction. He embraces reality and works through the pain, and gets to the other side. He uses his experience and strength to help others, and his past life of self-sabotaging behaviors has become his biggest asset. He has helped many young men because he understands their thinking and actions. More importantly, he understands the spiritual process of healing that he can now transmit with confidence.

He surrendered to his God the best he could and that made him receptive to all possible solutions. This translated into his being humble enough to follow the guidance of a mentor regardless of his reservations. I suggested he quit a lucrative job and move to the mountains, and he was willing to listen, surrender, and take action. He is a blessed guy. Too often when people begin to feel better, they take the reins of life back. Their surrender doesn't stick.

There's a woman I really admire: Her name is Kim. Her husband, Ron, had been a visionary and the first medical director at my place of employment. Kim went through hell and back with Ron until he got into recovery. He died with an eighteen-year recovery chip in his pocket at a conference in Puerto Rico.

Ron and Kim put together a spiritual principles lecture that they gave together a couple of times per month in our family program. I now have the privilege of doing that lecture with her. When we talked about how she got through the past few years after his passing, she explained that it was a combination of friends from her codependency recovery groups and her total willingness to surrender to God every day. She said, "Michael, I would have never survived [the grief] without my reliance on God." She is a courageous person who gained access to healing and power through surrender and willingness.

You have to be honest with yourself about your problems/issues/compulsions/obsessions and your inability to conquer them on you own. You can open your mind to spiritual principles and the existence of a power greater than yourself that can help you. You are invited to begin to recognize that in many ways you have been a manipulator.

Now the big task at hand is to surrender your life back to your Creator. I like the notion that God's gift to us is life and our gift to God is how we live that life. St. Ignatius, founder of the Jesuits—the priests who are the Navy SEALs of the Catholic church—wrote this prayer: "Take, O Lord, and receive my entire liberty, my memory, my understanding and my whole will. All that I am and all that I possess You have given me: I surrender it all to You to be disposed of according to Your will. Give me only Your love and Your grace; with these I will be rich enough, and will desire nothing more."

Ignatius is a good example of great things that come through surrender. He was a soldier who came from a noble family in Spain in the 1500s. He was wounded in battle and experienced a religious conversion while recovering. He gave his life to God, and millions of people have been helped by the example of his life and teachings.

His spirituality focused on the imitation of Jesus. Jesus was in constant conscious contact with his Father, forgave sins, healed the sick and mentally ill, and gave hope to the poor and marginalized. Ignatius believed we need to be constantly praying, that we need to be "in this world, but not of it."

There is an addiction recovery prayer that helps summarize Ignatius' philosophy. It says, "God, please put me in a position where I can be of most service to You and to Your children (all peoples)."

It is time for you to write a prayer wherein you give your life over to the care and protection of God—for real. Express this prayer with someone you trust or address it directly to your God.

It is not my job to try and convince you of the existence of the Divine within you. It is your job to wrestle with those questions/truths. Be kind to yourself—especially if you have experienced past traumas. Do the best you can. I like the saying, "Easy does it, but do it." Write a prayer and say it with your heart, emphasizing the giving of your life and will over to the care of your Higher Power. Say it every day (for the rest of your life, if you need to).

The best indicators of whether or not you have truly surrendered will come by your willingness to take certain actions, such as joining a community, getting a mentor, following directions, and proceeding with the inventory and amends processes. This whole deal continues to build on itself so do not stress about future actions, but do what you can today. Focus on today.

CHAPTER FIVE

Finding Your Tribe— Joining a Spiritual Community

"Trouble shared is trouble halved."

—Scottish proverb

There are certain sure indicators of authentic surrender. One is when you become willing to take specific actions you were unwilling to take in the past. You become willing to become "part of" a community, willing to obtain a mentor, and willing to follow direction (from someone who has been through the spiritual process of healing). This is true, regardless of where you are on your spiritual path.

It sounds so un-American to be totally reliant on anyone or anything outside of oneself; however, God reliance leads to freedom from reliance in all the other areas where we are unconsciously and unhealthily dependent. It is not easy for many—men, especially—to humble themselves and ask for help. It's hard to accept the need for community when you think you should be able to live life successfully without reliance on anyone or anything. Perhaps this unwillingness to ask for help, and the corollary need to be seen as independent and powerful, with its resulting stress, is what fuels the high rate of suicide among men ages twenty-five to forty-five.

Have you ever read a book or listened to a lecture and felt as though you'd received an amazing amount of insight? I have read many spiritual, self-improvement, religious, and psychology books that had good substance. The more I read, the more I would get excited and hopeful and think, *This is the answer to my life issues!* The excitement, though, fades quickly, and so does the practical application of the books' information or instructions. We have developed countless perceptions and attitudes that can't be fully corrected by the same device—our human brain—that caused the problem in the first place.

I heard someone say in a recovery meeting, "I don't go into my head [thinking] without a flashlight and a shotgun." A flashlight is to illuminate and a shotgun is to "shoot down" ideas that threaten my peace of mind. As we grow spiritually we can and do begin to trust our intuition, but we always need to remain in community, where we can let others see who we really are, where we can "tell on ourselves," and where we can be accountable. Others who know us can tell we are "off the beam" much more quickly than we can, because our distorted thinking processes have us going off-track—slowly and without our noticing—like the frog who gets boiled alive because he doesn't notice the water temperature slowly rising. Also, we have a strong tendency to delude ourselves. A healthy community and a mentor are vital to sustained and consistent growth and change.

Here are some reasons why we need community:
1. It is a way God can reach us.
2. It helps us to grow and change.
3. We learn about ourselves.
4. We learn love and tolerance.
5. We hear about ways to practice spiritual principles.
6. We acquire humility.
7. We find opportunities for service.

8. We reveal our true selves (people love us until we can love ourselves).
9. We receive acceptance from a place "where everybody knows your name."
10. We develop compassion for others upon hearing about their struggles.

I can't tell you how many times I have heard people say that they needed to hear exactly what was said or read at a twelve-step meeting, church service, or retreat. It seems as though God chooses to speak to us through other people. Obviously, God is everywhere, but there is something special about the intention of seeking God through, or in, community. Everyone has his or her past, wisdom, pain and sorrow, and (sometimes) hope to share. When we do this on a regular basis it becomes a part of our lifestyle—we understand that we need each other. As in our most intimate relationships, there are challenges that we face in community that both painfully and lovingly mold us into the person we are meant to be.

Community is where we learn about ourselves, both the positive and the negative. Did you know that when you are attracted to something you admire in somebody, it is because you have the capacity for that same quality inside yourself? Unfortunately, the same is true for qualities about people who annoy and irritate you. "If you spot it, you got it," or at the very least "If you spot it, then you had it." You only have a certain amount of knowledge about yourself, and the hidden sides (hidden even to you) are revealed throughout the process of being with people during the different seasons of your life.

I have been to thousands of twelve-step meetings, and there are always people at these meetings who present a challenge to me. Either they talk too much or they do not speak at all. They may have beliefs that do not jibe with my own. These people are the greatest teachers of love and tolerance. I like what Jesus says in Matthew 5 (43–47): "You have heard it said, 'Love your friends, hate your enemies.' But now I tell you, love your enemies and pray for those who persecute you, so that you may become the children of your Father in heaven. For he makes his sun shine on the bad and good people alike, and gives rain to those who do good and those who do evil. Why should God reward you if you love only the people who love you? Even tax collectors do that! And if you speak only to your friends, have you done anything out of the ordinary?" People whom we dislike, and who dislike us, present us with our biggest opportunity for spiritual growth. We will never "get there" or "arrive" at total perfection, but the striving toward the goal with God's grace is the point.

In recovery we are advised to put "principles before personalities." It's important for us to internalize this adage, because in order to grow spiritually we need to listen to the message and try to disregard whatever negative impression we have about the messenger. We need to listen for the spiritual principle so that we may learn to give and receive from everyone we encounter. We need to learn that it is not about circumstances and people but that it's what is going on inside of us and how we respond that make the difference in our spiritual life. Community is where we put spiritual principles into practice.

You need community more than community needs you. That is humbling. Think about any time you have left a job and wondered how the company would do without you. Usually, it does not take too long before everything is back to business as usual. Community will survive without you, but you will not do too well in life without being "part of" something larger than yourself, something besides your work and family. That is what life is about—living for something larger than you.

As you will read in later chapters, "You have to give it away to keep it." That's what they say in the rooms of recovery. You will get to maintain your new sense of purpose by being willing to serve others in some capacity. Taking a service commitment in your community of choice will have huge benefits like helping you feel a "part of." I have a minor service position at my church that helps me stay connected. Every six weeks or so I help set up the room and greet people as they arrive. Actually, I never look forward to it, but I am always grateful for the experience when it's done.

Sometimes the service position in the community or group will be the thing that gets you off the couch, into the car, and to the meeting or event. It is the sense of obligation that gets you there so you can be present to experience what is there for you. The task you were reluctant to perform or the meeting you didn't want to attend beforehand becomes the one you're glad you did afterward. The service position becomes the vehicle that saves you because it motivates you into action.

It is important that we let others love us in community. In the recovery rooms we say, "Let us love you until you can love yourself." But deep down too many of us have an underlying distorted thought process that says, "If you really knew me, you would not love and respect me." Community is the place where you confront these untrue beliefs about yourself. The closer you come to your true self, the closer you are to reality and happiness.

It is good to be known and accepted. A long-running and hugely popular TV show was set in a bar "where everybody knows your name." When people know you, they get to miss you when you don't show up. They can motivate you when you cannot motivate yourself. On the other hand, sometimes you will be the strong one who motivates others. Sometimes you will be the one providing the acceptance and encouragement. It is a basic human need to belong to a group of people. For those seeking spiritual fulfillment, belonging to a group of like-minded seekers is enormously helpful.

Being in community puts your life issues in perspective and helps you develop compassion for others. You can get too isolated inside your own head about your personal circumstances. Sit in on an open twelve-step meeting (meaning one where anyone—addict or not—is welcome). Listen to the sharing of the members. When you hear what others are walking through, sometimes with enormous courage and dignity, you will be inspired. Your own issues and challenges will almost seem like cherished offspring! You will be happy to go home to your own "problems." What a one-hour meeting can do to your perspective will trump days of trying to think your way out of your negative mind-set. Being in community is an intervention in your self-centeredness. You have to give your community of choice a true chance to work in your life.

I almost envy those who grew up in the era of my father: during the time when my dad grew up in Bay Ridge, Brooklyn, there seems to have been a stronger sense of community than we have nowadays. In his case, there was Catholic Mass, Catholic school, dances, and other social functions. Catholics like my dad identified with their parish church—just as others would identify with their own religious sect or denomination. The parish priest would even pray for the Brooklyn Dodgers during mass out of a sense of community. (Some of the same Dodger ballplayers would work in the neighborhood during the off-season, so they, too, were part of the community.) Things have changed as life has become more secular and many people have become more transient (especially in the United States). We have become more affluent, our homes more opulent, and our professions more white-collar than blue. Sadly, many people identify more with their professions, material possessions, and money today than with their community.

A Few Communities that Changed My Life for the Better

One of the best community experiences I've had was in a small mountain town in Colorado. I had just finished graduate school and was looking for my first job in the helping profession. One weekend during that spring of '95, while hiking in Rocky Mountain National Park, I was overwhelmed with a deep desire to live in such a place, in intimacy with nature. I longed to live in the mountains with the forests, trails, lakes, birds, and animals. Weeks later, I was playing golf with a man I knew well and another friend of his. My friend's friend asked me what I did for work. I told him that I was graduating and didn't know what I was going to do next. He put me in touch with a friend of his who managed an addiction rehab in Estes Park— in the very town closest to Rocky Mountain National Park. Although I had no previous intention at all of ever being an addiction counselor, I warmed quickly to the idea given the location of the center.

Things worked out and I ended up living there for nearly three years, working for the treatment center. I was single and new to the counseling field. Even though I had been semi-connected to twelve-step groups in Denver, to a church and a retreat center, nobody there really knew me because I had bounced around a lot and stayed on the edges of all those organizations. But in Estes Park, my community and social options were quite limited, which proved to be the best thing for me. There was nowhere to run and nowhere to hide.

In Estes Park I actively participated in a local twelve-step group for the entire time I lived there and continued to participate sporadically for the decade after relocating to the Denver/Boulder area. I made several lasting friendships and developed a passion for outdoor activities. My friends and I not only helped each other in structured meetings on a daily basis, but we also developed friendships with one another, which meant weekly coffee engagements, meals, and recreational activities. I would take long hikes in the summer and long cross-country skiing outings in the winter with my mentors and friends—Randy, a hippie from Berkeley, and Sal, an older, retired dean of a medical school who became my mentor. We would talk and process life for hours, which was exactly what I needed at the time. I developed a passion for hiking, snowshoeing, running, and snowboarding and was introduced to rock climbing, kayaking, and other sports.

It was not always tons of fun. In such a small community people would get on my nerves. My mentor, Sal, used to tell me when I'd be upset with all the nonsense that I'd hear in certain groups and fellowships, "Mike, remember why you're there." And that always stuck with me because I needed to remember that I was there to save my own bacon. I was there for direction and hope. I was there to get some perspective because I couldn't see clearly for all my emotions and thoughts. I needed to be redirected somehow. And the group itself was the intervention I needed on a daily basis. Just being there and listening and getting out of myself, getting out of my own way, getting out of my own thoughts and obsessions and compulsions and being able to just sit, contribute, listen, take it in—I was there to save my life.

Over time I developed true friendships with the people I met and reached out to in these twelve-step groups. I would pick up the phone and dial even when I didn't think the person necessarily wanted to hear from me. We got used to picking the phone up and saying hello or checking in with somebody. It helped me because when times got tough and there was a moment of crisis or weakness, I was able to call someone. If you're used to picking up the phone and talking to friends about your life (the good, the bad, and the ugly), the triumphs and the victories as well as the defeats, it will be much easier to reach out and call somebody in times when you don't want to. Those are the times when you usually need to call the most, and it's helpful to have developed the habit—it just becomes an automatic act and that's what ends up saving our bacon.

I had a buddy named Jason who owned a small resort in Estes. I met him in my spiritual group, and I ended up living with him for a while. We've been really good friends for nineteen years now, and he knows everything about me. I also know everything about him and we accept each other and love each other. It's great to know that there's somebody out there who knows everything about you and loves you and accepts you for who you are.

Jason had a big influence in my pursuit of my wife, and he helped me gain employment as director of counseling at a high school. God has used him greatly in my life. Now we talk at least once a week and he is like family to me. In recent years he has struggled and I have tried to be there for him. I always wanted a brother when I was growing up and God gave him to me. This was a direct result of my involvement in community.

There is one more story I would like to tell that illustrates one of the benefits of my involvement in the Estes Park community. After I left Estes I moved to Guatemala to learn Spanish. My wife came with me. When we returned we lived in Boulder for a year, then landed in Denver. I was working in a high school directing the counseling department, and in 2004 my wife was pregnant with our first child. Like most young fathers I had financial concerns. I knew that working in the high school was a good profession and I felt like I did some good work in that position, but I knew it wasn't necessarily where I was supposed to be.

I was motivated to provide for my family and I had a desire to move on to where I was really supposed to be next. I started the "visioning" process. I asked myself, "What is the one thing that I love?" At every job I ever had, even when I worked while attending schools (college or high schools) and inpatient/outpatient facilities—it didn't matter where—I seemed to gravitate toward the addicts, toward spirituality, and recovery. I always wanted to find the addicts and help them. So I said to myself, "That is probably what I am supposed to have as a full-time career."

I thought I needed to start applying to work in one of the world-renowned facilities, and that I would probably have to move my family. I wanted to get a job as a clinical coordinator or team leader in order to be able to help mold a team within a residential treatment center. My vision was to give the patients or the clients the best experience possible, the most love, the most acceptance, the most highly skilled clinicians, and assist them with the spiritual experience. I set that intention. I put together a letter with the intent to send it out to treatment centers with a positive reputation in the United States. With that intention in mind, I knew what I wanted to do.

One weekend around this time, we were up visiting my mother-in-law in Estes Park and I went to visit my old spiritual group. I was speaking with an oral surgeon (an acquaintance), and he asked me what I was up to. When I told him that I was working in a high school and that I was looking into different opportunities, he mentioned to me that he had a friend who was currently building a treatment center. Philip Anschutz had donated substantial funds to build the facility and he wanted a top-notch, world-class facility in the Rocky Mountain region that treated addiction and co-occurring disorders. My acquaintance said that they could use a guy like me. I immediately called Dr. Harmon. Within a short time, the place was built and I was hired. It turns out I was living just ten minutes from the hospital, yet I hadn't even known it was being built. We didn't have to move and my wife was very happy about that. I was able to jump into the field where I felt most comfortable and where I felt my real talents lay—leading a team within a residential addiction recovery center.

This led to my most rewarding employment experiences. It all started from being part of a community, showing up, and having a huge gift thrown in my lap. In twelve-step meetings throughout the world, people are encouraged to "show up" no matter how they feel. An old friend of mine would say, "Keep showing up until you want to show up." We're taught in the twelve-step rooms that you can't wait to "want to go" before you show up. You learn to take right action regardless of your thoughts and feelings. You give your wife that hug that she deserves and she needs in that moment, in that argument, in that moment of tension, then the emotion follows.

Here's an example that bears this truth out: At a funeral I attended back in Boston, I ran into a Jesuit priest, who remembered me from my Boston College (BC) days. He asked me what I was up to and I told him a little bit about my history, like getting kicked off campus after my freshman year for several alcohol-related incidents. I destroyed friendships and hurt the women I dated by being unfaithful. I was ashamed of my lack of effort to get the most from an opportunity that my parents had worked so hard to provide for me. I had regrets about the lack of positive contribution to the BC community. I spoke to him about my struggles with addiction, what had happened in my life, and who I was striving to be by God's grace.

Hearing this, he invited me to come back to BC to work with the incoming freshmen on addiction issues. I was to let them know a little bit about my story, what not to do, what to do if their friends had a problem, what to do if they themselves had a problem. Instead of taking a few weeks off to enjoy with my wife before another demanding school year began, I decided that this was the right thing to do. It was such a healing experience to be able to go back to BC and to be part of the solution and not part of the problem. It really repaired a lot of bad memories that I had. It all came out of the simple act of showing up when and where I needed to and being a part of it. It even launched my passion for public speaking.

In the past decade I have become involved in several communities that have helped transform my life. I have been part of a men's recovery group that addresses issues of intimacy, which meets a couple times weekly. Attending this group for years has revolutionized my life and has freed me on the inside and outside. I have watched the group go through many changes and phases and I have watched members come and go. I continue to attend no matter what because, as we say in the recovery world, "Meeting makers make it."

A guy I mentor told me that he did not feel connected to our men's group so I asked him to call two people from the group that day and share at the next meeting. He did so and he immediately felt more connected and "part of."

It is so easy to feel as though you do not fit in or that people do not care. That is when we begin to question the need for a group or community. Before long, we've talked ourselves out of attending, and—at first, anyway—we do not experience any negative consequences. Ultimately, we stop our association with the group altogether. I hear it all the time in the recovery world. It goes like this: "I stopped making calls," "I stopped going to my meetings," "I stopped praying, and then I relapsed!" Sometimes, relapse brings consequences like divorce, estrangement from children, and loss of self-respect. It all starts with disengagement from community.

My wife and I joined the same church because we felt that our individual spiritual journeys were too separate from each other. We tried many different churches before finding our current church-home. This church community has greatly enhanced our understanding of, and relationship with God. We go on retreat together every six months with about thirty other families, and what started out as associations have turned into friendships. We attend a weekly community group that has become something we look forward to and something our kids really enjoy. We feel a part of this community of extremely wounded people who need each other and God's grace. It is great to be around friends with whom we can comfortably discuss spiritual matters. We pray together, worship together, break bread together, and do service projects together.

What Types of Communities Could Help Foster Your Spiritual Journey?

The answer to this question can be simple when you're "lucky enough" to have a problem such as overeating, problematic sexual behavior, addiction, certain emotional problems, or when you're in a relationship with somebody who has an addiction or mental illness. There are tons of different twelve-step fellowships you can join in these cases. New fellowships rise up to address issues all the time, because the twelve-step model works. Do a Google search on your issue to find out if there is a twelve-step fellowship that can help you. If you have mental health issues such as depression or anxiety, many times you can find a therapy group to attend regularly. Voilà—instant potential community!

There are meditation groups such as those for centering prayer that meet weekly in many large towns and cities. There are church groups with some form of curriculum like a Bible study where people get honest with each other and pray together. I can't overemphasize the importance of having a spiritual group that meets at least once a week. Ask local mental health providers, religious leaders, or community volunteers for advice, or, if you are employed, talk to your employee-assistance plan or human resources professionals at the office; they may know of a group that's right for you.

There are lots of opportunities to connect through conferences, retreats, men's and women's groups—look for one that has a strong follow-up group component to foster community and constant growth. There has to be a fellowship component when developing relationships.

There are spiritual book clubs that can be a safe environment for people who may want to discuss their thoughts and applications of the books' content with like-minded people. With the Internet there are many ways to connect with others for these purposes.

It takes initiative, effort, humility, and determination to start your own group or to integrate into an existing one. It needs to be small enough so you do not get lost in the crowd but large enough to interact with a variety of people. Connecting spiritually is going to become the most important aspect of your life and community is one of the vehicles that will take you there. You cannot sidestep this task of finding a community and connecting with its members.

What to Look for in a Group and How to Set Up Your Own Group

Fortunately, there are groups that already exist that have an open-ended structure, which allow members to join at any time, and to leave the same way. Twelve-step meetings are structured so that newcomers are continually able to join existing groups, and the twelve-step groups form the model I will follow when discussing how a support community group may be set up.

Elements of an effective group include adherence to stated starting and ending times, that meetings are held on the days the organizers say they will be held (consistently), that they have some kind of organized structure (even a loose one), and that there is a member serving as leader, whether permanently or on a rotating basis. An established format or routine allows for the group's smooth functioning. And a ritual, which may or may not include formal prayer or meditation, should open and close the meeting.

An important part is that that there's no cross talk—that people are allowed to share their feelings and thoughts, pains, joys, and sufferings without the risk of being criticized or talked at, talked down-to, or lectured. Members should not interrupt or carry on side conversations, but respect the person who has the floor. Of course, there should be a suggested time limit for each person's sharing; in a forty-five minute meeting, for example, with five minutes each for the opening and closing rituals, there will be thirty-five minutes left for the topic reading (if there is one) and group sharing. If each member shares for between three to five minutes, then between six and ten members can share. The group leaders may gently remind long-winded members of the need to let the others in the group have their chance. The Native American tradition of using the "talking stick" can help members be attentive to one person at a time. In this tradition, only the person holding the stick can address the group, and he or she must pass the stick to another member when his or her sharing is up.

Having individuals with some prior group experience can be helpful in setting up your group, because they can bring their wisdom. It's always good to have newcomers with no experience as well, because they're usually more open and willing, and in many ways their participation adds vitality and spark to the meeting. So, in most instances, it's good to have people from all walks of life. We don't want to confine ourselves to just the country club crowd or just the crew that works at the factory. A group of the type I'm suggesting, based on a shared affinity, is at least in theory open to a diverse collection of members from all nationalities, ethnic groups, and socioeconomic levels—and that's great, because there is really something about the integration of all types of religious and political affiliations that brings a whole different dimension to the group. Everyone benefits. By the way, in a group like this, it's important to keep out any political and religious or theological talk. Make it the norm to focus on spiritual principles and experience, rather than opinions. A firm but gentle leader can accomplish this, especially one with experience.

Stay positive and accepting, look for the good, and look for the similarities instead of the differences between yourself and the other group members. Look for what you can give to the group, not what you can get out of it. And practice patience, love, and tolerance. Yes, it's great to enjoy the people whose sharing is always interesting and relatable, but you may learn more from the people who annoy you. Everyone has something to bring to the group. And you do, too. You have your life experience. Keep remembering that you and the other group members are not "bad people trying to get good," as it's said in the rooms of recovery. We're spiritually sick people trying to get well.

Creating community takes effort. The hardest part is taking those first steps and dialing that phone or showing up at the meeting place and walking in, not knowing anyone, sitting down, raising your hand, and saying, "I'm new." Often we have to have someone help us do that.

You could be a very competent businessman with a degree, a social standing, and a presence, yet still feel scared to death to go down to the local twelve-step meeting to get some help with addiction. There are often high levels of fear and a great deal of projection and judgment that we have over this process. I've heard countless stories about how people resisted, resisted, and resisted, and then finally made a decision to become a part of a fellowship— only to wish they had done it ten years earlier. They gained a sense of belonging, a sense of hope, fellowship, friendship, and direction. As a result of adding these fellowships to their lives, the hole started to fill.

Finding Your Tribe

So now you know what your next task is going to be. You need to identify between one and three groups or organizations that you will engage with over the next couple of weeks. It will be very important that you give these groups/organizations a true chance by attending the functions for at least three months before making a decision to leave (unless it is harmful or abnormally dysfunctional). Remember what they say in the rooms of recovery: "Go until you want to go."

Guess what is going to happen to you when you first think about joining a couple of groups. Your untrustworthy brain is going to tell you that you do not have the time, energy, or money to do anything more than what you are already doing. I am not asking you to lose sleep or spend less time with your kids. I am asking you to watch less TV and read fewer fantasy books or spend less time playing games on your computer. I am asking you to work out a deal with your neighbor or family member to watch your kids one night a week so you can attend the group. Ultimately, by taking time to care for yourself, you will be a more loving parent, a more productive and positive employee. It may seem counterintuitive, but I've seen it work.

There is never the perfect time to take this type of action, so just do it. Take the leap and go on the retreat or attend the conference or go to the meeting tonight. Take it one step further and introduce yourself to a couple of people and reach out, no matter how uncomfortable it feels. It might help you to look for somebody more uncomfortable than you are and try to give, rather than take. Pray before you go that your Higher Power guides your thinking and actions.

You may say you already have friends and don't need a group of this kind. But it is not enough that you have a few drinking buddies or 500 Facebook friends. Our souls yearn for a deeper connection with each other. Age, gender, political views, religious views, salary, and professions are not significant factors in this process. In fact it would benefit you to keep these things low on the priority list when looking for a group to join. What matters are your areas of wounding and your desire for positive connection.

If you are already a member of a few spiritually nurturing communities, then complete a gratitude list for each of these organizations. Focus your mental energy on what good this community has done in your life. Make a commitment to give back to it cheerfully. There is no perfect community because communities are comprised of people who are wounded. Maybe you are wounded, too, and accepting and being part of these organizations is a way for you to accept and love yourself as imperfect and in the process of becoming who you are meant to be.

If your community is sick, then ask yourself what you can do to be part of its healing and then do your part. It is much easier to judge than to take a risk. Life is short, so take the risk. Journal about it and share your thoughts and experiences with your mentor or trusted friend.

CHAPTER SIX

Everybody Needs an Uncle Jim

"The only gift is a portion of thyself."

—Ralph Waldo Emerson

This painful life requires that we accept the love offered to us by a loving and forgiving Father—the one who waits for us, who runs to us when we want him, and who is willing to totally forgive us and restore us to our place as His child.

In essence, this is what my Uncle Jim and other mentors have done for me. He invited me back home by accepting me, and gently mentoring me through some dark periods in my life. He is a big part of the reason why I know that God is Love: I have witnessed true, unadulterated love in him and sensed true holiness and connectedness to the Creator.

Uncle Jim has remained a hero to me throughout my adult life. There is always something that attracts me to him—his peace, his goodness, his serenity, his holiness, his acceptance, his insight, his joy of living, his unselfishness, and his sense of humor. You only get a call from Uncle Jim and the chance to experience him when you really need it, because he's one of those guys who is so "dialed in" to God that he only goes where he is most needed. He is a Jesuit priest who has truly given his life to God. He's never driven a car in his life, wears simple black and white clothing, and I think he cuts his own hair. He's a real New Yorker, a Brooklyn guy—in the best possible way.

There are numerous stories from people who have encountered him at retreat centers, high schools, soup kitchens, and homeless shelters who have told me that he profoundly changed their lives for the better. He is the antithesis of a status seeker. Once, he was scheduled to give a lecture at University of California, Berkeley, and when he showed up to speak they actually sent him to the soup kitchen nearby because he looked like one of the homeless people coming for lunch. So he went and had soup with the homeless and then came back and gave his lecture. He is the kind of priest you always want a priest to be—humble and good. His relationship with God is very personal.

One of my favorite Uncle Jim stories is about an interaction we had when I was new in recovery in 1991 and living in a studio apartment in Framingham, Massachusetts. I thought at the time that I was doing fairly well—but in hindsight I realize I was very depressed and scared. I didn't have any friends who didn't drink heavily and I didn't know what to do with myself. I wasn't particularly fond of my job and I felt stuck. One October afternoon I saw a movie called *Dances with Wolves*. The movie reminded me of how I had always wanted to be an Indian when I was growing up. I was always rooting for the Indians rather than the cavalry or the cowboys. So I went to see this movie, and when I came out I thought, *You know there is a better way to live. I don't have to wear a suit anymore. I think that I'm going to put in for my last month's rent and head out West, settle down on a reservation, maybe meet a woman, and go back to school or become a teacher and stick around on the reservation, learn the native language, and something great will happen.* I was crazy enough to do it.

I got a call from Uncle Jim out of the blue that day and he seemed concerned for me. *How does he know my number? What's going on? What does he know?* He said, "Mike, how are you doing? What's going on? What are your plans?"

I told him, "I'm thinking about quitting my job and heading out and driving across the country and settling down on the Lakota reservation." He started to question me by saying, "Well, Mike, you've been intoxicated for the last few years of your life. Do you think that it's the best idea to pack up now and head out when you're only about ninety days into the recovery process yourself?"

Then he told me a few stories about how St. Ignatius developed a process of discernment. It's an art form, and one of the indicators of healthy discernment is that the Holy Spirit will give your body peace if you are making a big decision and it's the right time for you. He asked me, "Mike, do you feel peace? When you think about going to the reservation, do you feel peace?"

I told him, "I don't feel peace; I never feel peace."

His response was, "Well, that doesn't mean that the decision is wrong. It just means that, as St. Ignatius would say, you need to delay. Since you don't feel peace, you need to delay the decision for a couple of months."

It was the first time in my life that I was scared enough to listen to another human being (other than when my sister directed me to my first twelve-step meeting). The results of following Uncle Jim's directions were uniformly positive. In the two months that I waited, I remained in recovery, going to twelve-step meetings and making a few sales at work. Remarkably, my company promoted me, gave me a car, and shipped me out West to the Denver office. They gave me a raise and I was able to settle in and take that opportunity. I saved some money, went back to graduate school, and even got to backpack throughout Europe. I really appreciate how Uncle Jim was able to slow me down without power tripping on me. He asked the right questions and gave me some gentle suggestions. And it altered my life.

Another time, when I had recently moved to Colorado and was living by myself, I was tormented, feeling like I shouldn't be dating or even be around women because I seemed to always leave them or hurt them. I acted out sexually in a way I had told myself I would never do. One night, I was lying on my bed filled with toxic thoughts. I was completely full of self-hatred and shame, so full of guilt and remorse that I couldn't even lift my head. Right then, the phone rang. It was Uncle Jim. He told me that I needed to look up. I did. Above my bed hung a picture of Christ, illustrated with the words of the gospels.

Uncle Jim said, "Look up and talk to your Higher Power. He came here to experience all the different human emotions and situations. And He knows what you are going through, He knows how you are feeling, and He wants to help you. You need to talk to Him." Uncle Jim encouraged me to do so and then gently hung up the phone.

The fact that Uncle Jim loved me unconditionally when I hated myself healed me more than anything. He spent many hours with me whenever I picked him up or dropped him off at his retreat house on Long Island before and after family gatherings. He would listen and gently advise me. He connected me with a retreat house in Sedalia, Colorado, that became a safe place for me to go during difficult times. He understood addiction, psychology, counseling, and spiritual direction, which is a powerful combination.

Uncle Jim experienced serious health complications over the past decade because he was one of the first responders in the 9/11 tragedy in New York City. He spent countless days counseling firefighters and others. During that time he inhaled toxic particles, causing him tremendous pain and discomfort. I thank God for this example of service in the face of suffering. I thank God for his mentorship, and for his love.

You may be reading all this thinking, "Great for you, Mike, that you have a near-saint in your family to see you through your tough times. My own family is as complicated as they get. There aren't any heroes in it." While I agree that I am very fortunate to know someone like my own Uncle Jim,

I've also been lucky to have several other mentors who helped change my life for the better.

In the late 1990s I went through a yearlong certificate program for the formation of spiritual directors. So many amazing things came out of that experience, but I think the best things were my connections with Cal and Jack. The program required me to give and receive spiritual direction throughout the process. The person I'd chosen to be my spiritual director did not work out, so I asked the director of the program for assistance, and she put me in touch with Jack. He ended up being my director for seven years (meeting monthly with me at a coffee shop) and I still meet with him periodically to this day. I met with him for years before ever discovering in a Google search that he had authored books on philosophy and that he was highly regarded in his field. He had been the chairperson for the joint PhD program for philosophy and theology at a well-regarded university.

There have been many times when a mentor has asked just the right question or has been there for me at just the right time that it was life-changing. I can recall an extremely painful experience that changed my life—a real hitting-bottom moment of truth. In the 1990s I had a series of unhealthy relationships and after each one ended, I would tell myself, "No more!" I would tell myself I was done with romantic relationships only to forget my declaration. This time, as usual, I subtly returned to the hunt for my next "hostage." Eventually, I found one.

Together she and I went on a wild ride for a few months. It ended when I realized that we were at disparate stages in our emotional and spiritual development and that I had done her a disservice. I had tried to make her dependent on me and she clearly did not need another man in her life to solve her problems. She needed true friendships with other women and herself and most important with her Creator. I stood in the way and I was using her in several ways. We drove down to Arizona to her parents' house, where I left her. When I did I felt sick, obsessed, and jealous—because I knew she would find someone else within a short time. I drove back to Colorado and met with my spiritual adviser in a twelve-step clubhouse. As he questioned me, I kept using the word "fool" so he probed by asking about my choice of words. I explained my history with romantic relationships and feeling like a fool, which I was able to trace way back into my youth. He kept asking questions that led to a flood of realizations.

Ever since I was a little boy I had been getting attention from women for being a bad boy. I remember getting sent to the principal's office in grammar school and I think the nuns felt sorry for me so they would give me soda or some other treat. Over the years of getting into trouble, I developed a sense of shame about being a person who did not quite measure up. Later in life nothing made me feel more ashamed than when I screwed up a relationship.

That day I experienced a profound realization. I saw my pattern with relationships as a form of self-sabotage that led to shame and self-hatred. Shame and self-hatred seemed like companions that I couldn't live without. I understood beyond the intellect that "my picker" was broken and it was not going to be repaired anytime soon. I was attracted to certain people for all the wrong reasons; all the self-knowledge in the world was not going to change that. I realized I was hopeless in the area of romance and God would need to pick my wife for me. I had always feared asking God for help when it came to romance because I secretly thought I would end up with some old, angry ex-nun. After all, God had more important things to worry about—not my desire for a wife and my ability to love.

But I asked God for help and left it with Him, or as the twelve-steppers say, "I let go and let God." I felt a certain amount of cathartic peace. I left my meeting with my spiritual adviser changed for the better in the area of intimacy. Within a few weeks of that experience I met my future wife in a restaurant (that's another story). After so many wrong picks on my part, my wife turned out to be the most beautiful person (inside and out). I'm still amazed at the paradox that total admission of defeat can lead to strength, liberation, and miracles.

My spiritual adviser mentored me by asking me the right questions and unlocking the truth inside of me. Seasoned spiritual directors have the skill to follow where the Spirit is leading and ask intuitive questions. He walked with me through several transitions including my meeting, courting, and marrying my wife.

Cal was a fellow student with me in the formation program. He is the pastor of a church. We started a spiritual direction group together. He turned from friend to mentor because he did our premarital counseling and continued to counsel us for several years into our marriage. When my Uncle Jim was unable to officiate at our wedding (because it was scheduled for the days right after 9/11), Cal was able to step in and perform the rites. From the very beginning of our marriage, Cal has been a mentor to us, earning our trust, which enables him to speak truth to both of us on many occasions. For example, he showed us how we both acted as though we were fighting for our lives with each other. That we were both constantly negotiating as if we were untrusting business partners reacting with fear. He taught us how to slow down and communicate more effectively with one another.

Over the past six years, Isaac has been my mentor. He took me through the spiritual steps of the addiction recovery program like a taskmaster and it was exactly what I needed. I had a spiritual awakening as a result of the process, and he met with me each week as I went through the Twelve Steps. He has been given a gift that he is willing to transmit to those who want it. There is something about this man that is so attractive—joy and freedom.

These days I usually meditate in a little chapel before our men's meeting. Many days, Isaac will slide into the chapel and we meditate together. I cannot tell you how many times he asks me how I am doing, and as I begin to talk he stops me after thirty seconds of my monologue and closes his eyes. He then proceeds to tell me exactly what I need to hear and do. He gives me very practical direction like, "Go hug Jill and tell her you love her." Simple, but I would not have come up with that no matter how long I would have thought about it. His life and messages have altered me forever. He has taught me to make connecting with God the primary focus of my life. I don't think that Isaac and I share the same religious faith, but he has helped me get closer to my God and myself than any person I have ever met.

I remember the first time I met with Isaac: I shared with him a little about my life situation and he scared me when he said, "Mike, you may not be ready for this." What he meant was that I might not be ready to totally give myself to the spiritual path. I got on my knees with him in the basement of his house and rededicated myself to God, and I was given the willingness to go to any lengths for victory over my addiction. I followed every suggestion he gave me with great success. For instance, he told me that I did not have the right message to transmit at that time, so I needed to let go of all the men that I was sponsoring. It was very difficult for me, but I listened. Actually, around a year later, on the day that I completed his assignments, a man asked me to be his sponsor! I have been blessed to mentor many men since, and these guys bring me great joy, friendship, and healing.

In the twelve-step programs I belong to, we call our mentors "sponsors." In the "real world" such guides are often called "mentors." You'll notice I have used both terms in this text so far. If you have a spiritual mentor in your life it is advisable that you use him or her consistently. If you don't yet have one, I strongly suggest you find one. Where are you going to find your spiritual mentor? If you are a member of a religious organization then it should be a little easier than for someone who is not connected to a spiritual community. But if you followed the suggestions in earlier chapters you should already be part of a spiritual community. In this case, you could be situated to look for someone who has been down the path longer than you. He or she does not need to be older than you—just more experienced in overcoming your particular problem or more advanced at utilizing spiritual concepts. He or she could be a small group leader or someone from your spiritual study group. Often the group's pastor, rabbi, or leader may have a few people who they can suggest. Sometimes it is actually the clergy member him- or herself.

There are many people like me who have been trained in spiritual direction or who have been through the Twelve Steps with a sponsor. Every twelve-step program follows the same basic steps, no matter the manifestation of addiction it addresses. The ideal situation is for you to find a recovering person with the same issues you have, who has dedicated him or herself to their spiritual practice, and has experienced a positive change in how they deal with life's struggles. I believe the greatest gift we have to give each other is using our redeemed wounds to help others with the same or similar wounds.

There are many trained individuals who give direction (sometimes spiritual in essence) for a living. Many counselors and life coaches understand the spiritual path to recovery. There are therapists who even facilitate groups and individual sessions that focus on the important reflective questions of life. This gives people the opportunity to seek the truth within themselves with the guidance of another person.

There are many forms of trauma and many therapists trained in various forms of trauma therapy. For example, there is trauma from growing up in an alcoholic home and not receiving the right kind of love and nurturing necessary for healthy development. Many individuals have been violated sexually or experienced physical or emotional abuse. There are those who experienced their parents' death or divorce at a critical developmental time in their life. We react to life through the filters of our trauma and we don't even realize it. When the trauma is healed, we are able to progress spiritually. Until then, many people get stuck and feel as though they are in a rut.

Life coaches can help you explore your desires and goals for spiritual development and hold you accountable to the process. I have several friends who have business mentors who they pay as a consultant but use as a life coach, because when it comes down to it, most personal transformation can be considered spiritual. Anytime we are focusing on being a better and more fulfilled individual and we are humble enough to ask for help, it becomes a spiritual process.

There are plenty of business coaches and consultants who fully understand and live according to the principles of honesty, hope, and faith that help individuals toward constant transformation and success. The important thing is that you have one-on-one contact with this person. There needs to be openness over time to reveal your true self, and remain open to the risk of being judged. There needs to be a willingness to ask for guidance and follow suggestions. You need to be willing to initiate the conversation—not just the first time, but every time—because they are not asking you for help, you are asking them.

Everyone has his or her own style in the mentoring process; the results are the true indicator of the overall effectiveness. As Jesus said, "You will know them by their fruit." When someone leads you to the truth about yourself and helps teach you how to live by correct spiritual principles, then your inner life should improve dramatically. The mentor is just doing his or her life dance, and whether you follow along or not is your choice. Ultimately, God is the transformative power that originates and manifests itself in your life. The mentor is the vessel and guide—not the one causing the healing.

This is not an aspect of the process that can be eliminated no matter what your circumstances are. I suggest you pray—even if you do not believe in prayer or God—for the willingness, direction, discretion, circumstance, insight, and courage to identify a mentor. Ask for help within the next seven days; procrastination is a killer. Fear, shame, and pride will try to stop you from getting spiritually well. Pride will tell you that you do not need to go to this length for victory. Fear will tell you that people will think less of you or do not have the time for you. Shame will tell you that you are not worth it. Grandiosity will tell you that you already are a great mentor and that people should live as you do. Life is too short to wait for the perfect time and place to reach out to another person.

My own perspective is that men should reach out to men and women should reach out to women, unless one is gay. The sharing and intimacy of an opposite-sex mentoring relationship can lead to a blurring of boundaries between two people who may develop sexual feelings toward each other. This would defeat the purpose of the mentorship and can create other problems, so I suggest that those of you reading this follow these guidelines, which were discovered by those in the rooms of recovery. Why reinvent the wheel? (However, I have seen gay individuals work with the same sex and the opposite sex with success, so it is whatever works best.)

I heard a guy in a twelve-step meeting say, "The reason I have a sponsor is because my brain is out to kill me and make it look like an accident!" My own belief is that God gives us the ability to truly help others, in the sense that God chooses to use us as his hands and feet. Ironically, though we have been given this ability to help others, the one person we cannot help is ourself by ourself.

The best advice I've heard on selecting a mentor comes from the rooms of recovery as well. I tell people what others have told me: Find someone about whom you can say, "I want what he or she has." I'm not referring to their spouse, their fine home, or new car; I'm referring to their sense of self, their peace, their joy and happiness. If I want what you have, then I will be willing to do what you do.

Bill Wilson (founder of the Twelve Step movement) had a mentor named Fr. Ed Dowling, SJ from St. Louis, whom Bill considered his spiritual sponsor. Fr. Ed was not an alcoholic, but he understood addiction and depression and he was a great supporter of the nascent recovery movement. In 1952, Bill gave Fr. Ed a Christmas present, which was a leather case with the prayer of St. Francis inside. When Fr. Ed died, this leather case and Christmas card went to his niece.

Fr. Ed's niece gave it to my friend and mentor Fr. Dick because she felt that a Jesuit in recovery needed to have it. When Fr. Dick was diagnosed with Stage 4 lung cancer, his superior moved him back to a Jesuit home at the University of St. Louis. Before Dick left Colorado, he gave me the leather case with the prayer inside. It is such an amazing feeling that I am part of this legacy of mentorship and love, and of one fellow sufferer helping another. I will always cherish that gift.

I have a young friend named Ray. His sister came through my treatment center years ago and he would come back to see me for lunch when he was in town from college. This continued while he was in law school and then in a career. He struggled with the true nature of his own problems for years. He always went to psychiatrists, wanting them to medicate away the anxiety and depression caused by his thinking and actions. It was years before he was able to accept the fact that he was an addict.

I had not heard from him for quite a while; with most of the guys I mentor, this either means he is doing really well or really poorly. One day I decided to check in with him by sending him a text. To my delight, he was four months clean and going to twelve-step recovery meetings in addition to seeing professionals. I texted, "You rock!" and he texted back, "No, my sponsor rocks." That was music to my ears. He had asked someone to be his mentor and he said he never felt better in his life after following his mentor's direction.

Best wishes to you for this somewhat scary and humbling part of the journey. You will not regret it. Your sponsor/mentor does not need to be perfect. Just be prayerful, willing, and ready to take action. You will be giving your sponsor/mentor a bigger gift than you now realize. You are giving him or her an opportunity to get out of him or herself, and to be of service.

CHAPTER SEVEN

Getting Right
with Yourself

"How can you say to your brother, 'Let me take the speck out of your eye,' when all the time there is a plank in your own eye?"

—Matthew 7:4

M ost humans have a perception problem and are truly unaware of many aspects of their feelings, motives, and actions. We can clearly see the wrongs of others, but have trouble identifying the role we have played in a given situation ourselves. We are somewhat aware of our negative contribution in any given situation or relationship, but we are much more focused on others as the real problem. There is no question that thousands of problems in this world exist and that people hurt each other, directly and indirectly. But you are attempting to experience life differently and to find peace and happiness, which requires a certain type of self-examination.

As you uncover the truth about yourself and discard all of the faulty perceptions, you are invited to begin to discover your true self. You will be challenged to identify the good, the bad, and the ugly about the "real you" and to let go of the negative and build on the positive. The task of completing an inventory of your life is an action that will bring humility, truth, and perspective. You will be able to wipe the dirt out of your eyes and see clearly. When that happens, when thoughts and feelings are unobstructed, you will feel comfortable and secure within. You will understand who you are.

There is a Native American prayer I particularly like:

> "Oh, Great Spirit, whose voice I hear in the wind,
> Whose breath gives life to all the world.
> Hear me; I need your strength and wisdom.
> Let me walk in beauty, and make my eyes ever behold the red and purple sunset.
> Make my hands respect the things you have made and my ears sharp to hear your voice.
> Make me wise so that I may understand the things you have taught my people.
> Help me to remain calm and strong in the face of all that comes toward me.
> Let me learn the lessons you have hidden in every leaf and rock.
> Help me seek pure thoughts and act with the intention of helping others.
> Help me find compassion without empathy overwhelming me.
> I seek strength, not to be greater than my brother, but to fight my greatest enemy: myself.
> Make me always ready to come to you with clean hands and straight eyes.
> So when life fades, as the fading sunset, my spirit may come to you without shame."

The most important line for me is this: ". . . to fight my greatest enemy: myself."

Obstacles to Happiness

What is blocking you from peace, happiness, and inner freedom? What causes most of your inner disturbance? In the addiction recovery movement, many of us believe that the "sunlight of the spirit" gets blocked by resentments, fears, sexual/relationship issues, unresolved trauma, character defects, and secrets. Such hang-ups may keep one in a self-constructed prison of self-centeredness. When you have a bad toothache, you become "tooth-centered" until the pain goes away. It's all you can think about. When you are "self-centered," you become spiritually sick. It's natural to seek some form of escape from yourself in that situation. Consider the following inventories that invite you on the journey to inner freedom.

Resentment Inventory

This is where the writing and soul searching begins, and this is a beautiful process. For supplies, all you need is a notebook and a pen. Then you begin to look at your resentments.

The word "sentiment" comes from the Latin word *sentir*—to feel. Thus to *re*-sent is to re-feel, and re-sentments are re-feelings. Often, our resentments stem from hurts—perceived or real—that others have caused us. Whether the hurt you did me is real, or whether I have misinterpreted some action of yours that hurt me, holding on to a resentment against you for a hurt I believe you have caused me only hurts one of us—me. There is a saying about holding on to resentments: "It's like swallowing poison and hoping the person who hurt you will die."

Open your notebook. Begin by putting a prayer at the top of the page, a prayer asking that your God will help you to see the truth. There is not a right or wrong thing to put on the resentment inventory. If a thought comes to mind, do not question it—get it down on paper. If need be, fill up a whole page with names of people who have hurt you, annoyed you, angered you, and so on.

Then think about why you are angry or hurt. What's the cause? For example, "She hurt me because she cheated on me. She went behind my back and she lied to me. She is untrustworthy." Put down on paper why you have negative feelings toward this person—or institution. Haven't you ever had resentments toward institutions like collection agencies, car dealerships, or the IRS? Write them down. Be as blunt as you can. Honesty is essential. It's not about length. Don't scratch where it doesn't itch, but pray that pride and denial will not hinder the process. You may have ten resentments or you may have 110 resentments—the number is not important.

The third part of the process of creating a resentment inventory is to figure out how that person or situation affected you. Did he or she affect your ambitions, personal relations, self-esteem, emotional security, physical security, financial security, sexual relations, or personal relations? There will be fear behind most of these "-securities." When anything threatens one of your instincts—instincts that are God-given—you may become fearful and form resentment. We all have certain instincts for love, affection, shelter, food, survival, and sex. Every human being has basic instincts. When these human instincts start to run your life, when you want more than your fair share of affection or more of your fair share of anything, relationships begin to break down.

I often hear recovering addicts say, "My drug of choice is 'more.'" When your instincts start to dominate you, you want more of whatever it is you want. It might be something as apparently benign as financial security. A typical, resentment-driven reaction might be, "If you get between me and my money, I think you're trying to rip me off." If you think that way, you will go into instant resentment mode.

Here is a very short example of what a resentment inventory could look like:

Resentment—Person or Institution	The Cause	Affects My	My Part
My boss	Promised promotion; never came through	Self-esteem	Lied on expense reports
		Financial security	Passive-aggressive; said yes to projects then blew them off
		Ambition/fear	
	Criticizes me in front of staff; intimidating	Emotional security	Bad-mouthed him

Take a look at the fourth column. Have people done you wrong? Of course.
Can you change that? Probably not. You and God are the only team that
can transform your perceptions. So keep the focus on you; never mind what
others did or didn't do, just focus on your part in the resentment. This is
what will give you freedom. You're not letting all these people who have
harmed you off the hook by doing this; you're accepting that it may not be
up to you to hold them accountable. But you have to evict them from your
head and your heart.

Remember, "The truth will set you free. But first, it will piss you off." This
process takes a lot of courage, but you need to ask, "What's my part?" A
lot of times you find it is your selfishness, dishonesty, fear, and self-seeking
behaviors. Selfishness means that "I want what I want." Being self-seeking
means "I want to look good." Your resentment inventory may well
uncover patterns of jealousy, envy, bitterness, self-pity, playing the victim,
expectations, judgment, blaming, entitlement, dependence, domination, etc.

As an example, let me describe one of the hundred resentments that I had
in the early 1990s when I first went through this process. (It will also give
you a glimpse of how insane my thinking was.) I had a lot of resentments
against certain types of guys. Specifically, while growing up in New York, I
was always getting into fights with big, seemingly angry Italian-American
men. When I left for college in Boston, I thought such problems were
behind me, because as I envisioned Boston, it consisted of legions of Irish-
Americans drinking and having fun—no fights with angry, Italian-American
New Yorkers. (I guess I had never heard of Boston's North End, which is the
traditional home of many Italian Bostonians!)

Guess what? When I arrived in Boston, I discovered I had brought both my
best friend and my worst enemy with me: myself! I finally said to myself,
"Hey, I'm an insecure guy, and I use women to validate myself. I like to
make them laugh and I flirt with them. When I'm intoxicated I need a lot
of attention. I have a big mouth and I flirt with girls who happen to have
large boyfriends who tend to get angry when you mess with their girlfriends.
Some of those large boyfriends are Italian. So there's a good chance I'm
going to end up in a fight with a large Italian guy." I started to see this

correlation between being an insecure flirt and the number of bruises I had sustained at the hands of large, angry Italian men in bars.

In the past twenty years, I haven't had any issues with large Italian guys. It was my attitude, my drinking, my mouth, my insecurity, and my flirting with unavailable women that created the problem. By creating your own resentment inventory, you may start to see patterns, often involving selfishness, fear, dishonesty, pride, blaming, playing the victim, expectations, greed, and so on.

You may also start to recognize cognitive distortions such as "mind reading." Maybe that guy really wasn't scowling at you; maybe he just had a headache. Awareness of your own resentments and the part you (and your distorted thinking) play in them can help you not only understand others better (and thereby get along with them better), but it can also help you understand and change your own behaviors that are not serving you well.

The Fear Inventory

The fear inventory is similar to the resentment inventory. Fear can be dangerous. Many people unconsciously act on their fears. You have to understand your fears to learn what lies behind them. As with the resentment inventory, it helps to get it all down on paper. You may want to look at fear as including concern, worry, or anxiety.

"I am concerned what people will think if I quit this job and go back to school."

"I am afraid he will leave me if I risk sharing my true feelings."

Many times you have to ask yourself, "Why do I have this fear?" When a friend of mine went through this process, she had an intense fear of losing her boyfriend.

"Well," her mentor said, "Why do you have that fear?"

She said, "Well, John might be the only one for me."

The mentor said, "Why are you scared of that?"

She said, "Well, if he's the one, then there's not going to be anyone else, and I'll be lonely."

"And why are you scared of that?"

"If I'm alone and lonely, I'll relapse back into my old promiscuous behavior, and I'll be miserable, and I'll be abandoned, and I'll have a horrible life," she said.

So she was able to see that the fear wasn't about losing her boyfriend. The fear was abandonment, being left alone, and being unloved. She was able to work through the fear, as well as deal with some of the abandonment issues that she needed to address before moving on with her life.

There are usually many more layers to the fear and distorted beliefs underlying your stated fears. You have to get to the bottom of them and accept that you can't get rid of fear on your own. You need to engage your Higher Power in that process. Your Higher Power can help you walk through the fear, rather than trying to run from it or fight it—because neither of those work.

I remember when I was in graduate school I suffered from the "imposter syndrome." I believed the school had made a mistake by accepting me into the program. I thought I'd best keep a low profile, not wanting for them to catch on until I had my degree. One day a professor confronted me, asking why I never participated in class discussions. I was forced to look at my fear. I put public speaking and group participation on a fear inventory. I asked myself why I was so scared to speak. And scared is what I was: my throat would dry up, my face would turn red, I'd stutter, shake, and be unable to make eye contact.

I prayed and went into my heart for the answer. I realized that I had decided around the age of eight that I was stupid when I was having difficulty reading. I decided that there was something wrong with me, and people would know it if I spoke up in class. I had low self-esteem, so I cared more about what others thought of me than about what I thought of myself. The underlying fear was that I would be exposed and be judged in a negative light.

I gave the fear up to my Creator the best I could at the time. Soon, I found myself in an internship in which I needed to give talks and speak in front of others. I would get on my knees in the bathroom and pray that God would take away my fear and work through me. Not long afterward, I found myself speaking in front of crowds of up to 800 people with courage and humor.

It is amazing what this combination of action, surrender, and reliance on a Higher Power can do for one's life. Pain—in the form of fear in this case—is a powerful motivator. I was able to walk through to the other side of the fear, instead of running from it or trying to conquer it. I was able to see that reliance upon a Higher Power equals courage and so one of my biggest fears became one of my biggest gifts.

Set up your fear inventory the same way you set up your resentment inventory, but only in three columns. Start with a little prayer at the top of the page. Then list your fears. Are you afraid of going into a meeting? Are you afraid of looking for a new job? Maybe you're afraid of getting into a relationship—or out of one. You might be afraid of people finding out who you *really* are. You could be afraid of being vulnerable. There are a thousand concerns or fears you may have. There's a lot of fear in many of us. List your fears. They will immediately start to be less frightening.

Once your fears are listed, select one to "inventory." Write the name of the fear in the first column. In the next column, write about where the fear comes from or why you have the fear. As an example, let's suppose you fear taking risks. You believe you are in fear of taking risks because "others will judge me."

Fear	Why do I have it/Where does it come from?	Did self-reliance fail me?
Public speaking	Belief that I am not smart and people will judge me	Yes
Writing a book	People will be highly critical	Yes

The most important part of this process involves taking the risk to trust your Creator and placing the fear in God's hands. As you pray for the fear to be removed, you may ask God to direct your thinking. When this process is put into practice, this translates into courage.

When I was dating my wife I would pray before seeing her: "God, please take away my fear and help me be myself, direct my attention to what you would have me be." By acknowledging my fear and petitioning for its removal, I gained mastery of my fear.

Relationship/Sex Inventory and Sexual Ideal

Next is the relationship/sex inventory process. Here you will take a look at your relationships and how you've acted and reacted in them. You need to be willing to explore where you've gone wrong in your relationships.

A "sex inventory" isn't a list of notches on a bedpost or a list of conquests, although it can involve a close look back at everyone with whom you have been sexual. However, what you are looking for is not quantity, but quality—specifically the quality you brought to the relationship(s).

Were you manipulative, either using sex to get love or love to get sex? Or was the main quality you brought to the relationship that of jealousy, a feeling of insecurity that made you want to control your partner? As you write the names of your partners and the wrongs you feel they have done you in the column format, take a good look at the last column, and be honest about what your part in the resentment or other relationship problem was. You may find that you have been fearful, selfish, manipulative, or jealous, and I'm willing to bet that's not really the way you want to be in your future relationships. Once you have seen the qualities you don't want to bring to present or future relationships, you are on the road to successfully changing your behavior.

You need to look at who you want to be in your current relationship or who you want to be in a future relationship. When you understand the qualities you hope to embody, you can work toward them. Examples might include generosity, passion, commitment, and a willingness to listen and work through problems.

I remember when I thought I had met "the one" after a three-hour conversation. She was a nice Southern, Christian girl and I had met her at a business conference. I was in my first year of recovery from addiction and I was looking for an easy way out of taking responsibility for my life. Within a couple of conversations with her, I decided we were extremely compatible, and I thought she was looking for someone to love her, too. I went to a twelve-step meeting and told one of the participants—an older guy I could be honest with and who would be just as honest with me—about the relationship. I added that I was thinking of moving down South to be with her. He turned the idea over in his mind for a moment. Then he said, "You'd better break up with that girl quickly. She's crazy." I was a bit taken aback.

"I haven't even told you her name or anything about her," I blurted out.

He looked at me in the eye and said, "Any woman who's attracted to you at this stage of your life is crazy."

I thought about it and realized he was right. You are attracted to—and you attract—someone who is where you're at. So if you think you're more evolved than your spouse or your friends or whoever—it's not true. It doesn't mean you and your partner are alike; it means that you function at the same level of emotional sickness or health. If you're going to grow and have healthier relationships, you desperately need to grow spiritually. You need to envision a healthy ideal to grow toward. Then you can attract and be attracted to what your heart desires. Then you can grow with that person.

Asset Inventory

At times, looking at fears, resentments, and relationship issues can become discouraging. You need to identify and own your assets because they are part of who you are as much as your deficits. You were made by God, and God doesn't make junk. What gifts were you given? Is it that you love people or that you're a good listener or that you're always there for others? In compiling your asset inventory, feel free to get feedback from friends and family, because often others can see you better than you can see yourself.

Secrets

Secrets are another important thing to put down on paper, especially things about yourself or your actions that you would rather take to your grave. Secrets are like mushrooms; they thrive in the dark. But you want to live in the light, so secrets have to go. Sharing secrets can be difficult, but with a trusted mentor, you can do it. You will find that when you open up and let the light of day shine on your secrets, it will be like putting down a heavy burden. You may even discover that your secret isn't as secret as you thought. You may find that you are not as bad as you thought you were. Remember, if there's a name for the thing you've done that you are keeping secret, it means someone else has done it, too. That thought can give you the strength to share your secrets with another, which will help to set you free.

Once you've completed your inventories (resentments, fear, sex, and secrets), you will move to the next phase of your development. It's been a lot of work, but well worth it—so much so, I'd argue, that a human being's time couldn't be better spent. The inventory process creates a tremendous amount of self-awareness, and reveals what has been blocking you from your own happiness, from others, from yourself, and from God. These resentments, fears, and intimacy issues have blocked your heart and spirit.

The whole act of writing out each inventory is an incredibly enlightening process. All it takes is a notebook and pen and some willingness, a prayer at the top of the page, and a little guidance from someone who has been through this process him- or herself. You find these people in any twelve-step meeting, but you can also find them in any religious tradition, because moral inventory—no matter what name it goes by—seems to be a universally recognized tool in the process of spiritual healing.

CHAPTER EIGHT

Transparency and Vulnerability

"Nothing is so oppressive as a secret . . ."

—Jean de la Fontaigne

It is so important for everyone to have at least one person in his or her life from whom nothing need be kept secret—including thoughts, emotions, past actions, shames, resentments, guilt, fears, secrets, character defects, hopes, dreams, and aspirations. Since most people suffer from the imposter syndrome, we all need someone to know and accept us at our core.

The next task is for you to take your inventory to your mentor, pastor, rabbi, or a trusted and close-mouthed friend who understands the value of confession. In my own life, this process began in Framingham when I wrote down everything that I could about my life. I was twenty-three at the time; it was 1991, probably three months after my spiritual experience in the Jeep on Route 9. I drove down street after street looking for a Catholic Church; I knew that each Catholic Church has a rectory, where the priest lives. I found one, banged on the door and as it flew open, I began to blurt out my story—my "confession" as Catholics would call it—and getting everything off my chest all at once, in tears.

The puzzled guy who had opened the door looked at me and said, "I just need you to know that I am not a priest—but this is incredible!"

He added, "I am becoming a priest, but I'm not one yet, so I cannot give you absolution."

"Please sit down and listen," I asked, and he did, so I just went off. I told him everything. At the time that's what worked for me, I gave it to a complete stranger, and that's all I was able to do.

Over time and in my spiritual journey over the years, I've on occasion found the need to do these inventories—but now I bring them to a trusted friend or mentor when I do. Some of these are in-depth inventories, and some are less so, but the layers of the onion continue to come off and I get new insights by sharing them with a friend who can help me look at my own part in things; that's the only part I can change, and that's the part I find that is so hard to look at on my own.

There is something magical that happens, something that is freeing about this process, so that when we come out of it we feel more comfortable in our skin. We start to be able to look ourselves in the eye, to look in the mirror, and accept and like what we see. The void inside of us dramatically shrinks, so there is no urge to fill it with chemicals or any other God substitute. Hopefully you can see the necessity of this task, but even if you don't yet recognize the need—please do it anyway.

It's very freeing to be able to tell another person what I'm dealing with or what I'm thinking, or how upset I am with a situation. You need to have the right people around you—ones who won't sit at the bar and give you another drink and tell you, "Forget her; she's no damn good anyway. You need to get out of that relationship." If you're around the right people, they'll always lead you back to yourself and your own issues, encouraging you to look at the way you're seeing things and what your part in it is. They'll listen and they'll be kind, but a good friend knows that the issue doesn't lie outside of yourself, but within you. And they'll always lead you back to that fact. These people become angels, lifesavers, soul mates; they provide part of what we've always been looking for in life—unconditional love and acceptance.

My wife has attended the same women's group for years, where she has made some true and deep friends. When she and I were experiencing difficulties, she would do her own inventory and bring it to her group, where she was able to get perspective, feel heard, and be comforted, all at the same time. Her friends did not fuel the fire but empathetically listened and carefully gave her honest feedback. Obviously, it's important that the people you choose to practice transparency with have honesty, integrity, and insight.

This part of the journey is like coming out of the water after being submerged for way too long. It is the inner freedom that every human being yearns for and does not know is available.

It's a great feeling not to have to compare yourself to others anymore. This person is a great golfer. That person is a great speaker. She's good-looking. He's really smart and successful and makes a lot of money. There's no need for comparing when you're free inside and you know that everybody has their assets and liabilities and everyone's doing the best they can—including you. And so other people do not intimidate you anymore because you're not as concerned with them. After all, all you know of them is their outsides— what you're concerned with is them and their insides. I may be an Irish-Catholic guy from New York who drank too much and has problems with intimacy and I think I have nothing in common with the business guy from California. But once you get inside, to the heart of a person, you start to realize that everybody knows shame, everybody knows guilt, everybody knows insecurity, everybody knows fear, everybody knows regret, everybody knows guilt. Everybody knows hurt *and* sorrow *and* anguish *and* crushed dreams *and* obsession *and* compulsion *and* disappointment. You realize that once we get underneath the surface and we start to talk about what's true and about what's real inside of us, we find out that there are so many more similarities than there are differences. Many times you're able to see the truth. It's an amazing experience to go through this process—afterward you could even sit and talk to a movie star and be comfortable in your own skin and feel no need to impress him or her, or feel any type of intimidation or need for comparison.

I always wanted to rise to the top of the heap, to be the captain of the team. Or I wanted to hide in the back of the classroom. I didn't know what it was like to be a person among persons—just in partnership with someone, part of a team. It was undesirable for me to look at it that way. It's been an amazing experience to be continually transparent and to talk about what's going on with me and to get things down on paper and to see things clearly and to be able to discuss that with another individual and to hear others do the same. It's an amazing gift you are given when you go through this process.

It's when we have been through this process and we are able to guide someone else through it that the magic really happens. That's where the real joy happens, sitting there listening to someone else get free and listening to their story and helping them step away from hell one inch at a time. You may not have experience with the subject they are choosing to disclose, but you will understand the feelings underneath. You, for instance, may like your job and your friend may disclose how frustrated he is in his position or place of employment. You will be able to listen and relate because you know frustration in other areas of your life. If you cannot relate at all to what someone's saying, then don't try—it is insulting, especially if someone has experienced a significant death or divorce. That is a time to listen and walk with the person through the situation. Sometimes just "being" with a person is all that is required.

There will be times when you will be embarrassed or people will let you down and break your trust. But if you live this way in order to honor yourself and grow spiritually, then you will ultimately benefit from this practice. Transparency is much harder for some than for others. The more difficult it is, the greater the long-term reward. Your Higher Power knows your heart. I like the saying, "Faith can move mountains, but you better bring a shovel." We need to do our part to avail ourselves of the gifts that await us. Taking the risk of being transparent is one way to develop the self-acceptance that will come from this lifestyle.

There is the person who will hear your inventories and a couple of close-mouthed friends, but what about the rest of the world? I think that talking about politics, sports, real estate, the economy, the weather, travel, education, and religion are all fine in the right context. In order to develop deeper friendships and associations, you will need to take some risks. You can start by sharing your feelings, thoughts, or experiences, because this is a form of vulnerability that can lead to another person relating to you. Your sharing could give someone the opportunity to share as well; you could help to heal someone else by helping yourself. Give it a shot and know that your Higher Power is truly with you.

Here is the crazy thing: Most people will actually respect you more the more you reveal about yourself. Sometimes when someone gets totally real it is refreshing and you feel more connected to him or her. In order to feel clean inside I suggest having a few good friends that you can totally get honest with. That is what my buddies like Dan and Stan were to me in early recovery. They were true friends that I could disclose anything to, and I did. All along the journey there have been trusted men in whom I've confided. They have helped save me from myself.

Hopefully you will learn from your self-inventories that you have more "issues" than you realized before you picked up this book. If you are anything like me, then your knowledge of these areas of weakness does not make them go away just because of your insights or efforts to expel them. Here are some very common shortcomings: selfishness, fear, resentment, playing the victim role, self-pity, shame, grandiosity, procrastination, dishonesty with self and others, lust issues, control issues, dependency issues, unhealthy attachments, insecurity, narcissism, gossip, greed, envy, jealousy, etc. The list is unending and you will see a few patterns emerge when you disclose your inventories to your mentor. The first layer of the onion will come off on your journey to your core. Some of these "character flaws" will never totally leave you, but you will receive a reprieve at times based upon grace and your spiritual growth (your dedication to the process). My friend Shaun would pray for protection from his defects of character every morning when he asked for another day of recovery. One of the ways in which you will diminish the power of your personal flaws is through your openness to share these consistently and as often as needed to get relief. Many cultures have the saying that a problem shared is a problem halved. Bill Wilson said that we are not related to each other out of our virtue but we are tied together by our defects and our struggles to overcome them.

Whatever your struggles are within, you will eventually be your own gift to humanity once they are surrendered and you work through the process of healing. I like Henri Nouwen's concept of the wounded healer: Our personal transparency can be part of the healing process for others as well as ourselves.

I love twelve-step meetings because they are a place of transparency. If you have not been to a meeting, then pick an "open" meeting to go to (one that admits members of the general public, not just addicts). As they say in most any of the numerous fellowships, "Take the cotton out of your ears and put it in your mouth." If you truly listen and experience the transparency you find there, you will be positively affected. We are all connected in some way to each other. If you are given the grace to see and hear the similarities rather than the differences, you will slowly become "a part of" because you, too, will eventually let down your guard and accept the fact that you belong (to the human race, which is, after all, quite flawed).

This is all about growing up and working on your character. For example, let's say you like to gossip. Eventually, you will get sick and tired of having to reveal to others the fact that you are a gossip, and you will become aware of the pain that you cause for yourself by gossiping. Remember, we are not punished *for* our sins but *by* our sins. These shortcomings are actually a form of self-punishment. When you start to get that fact, then you will start asking God for help. The help many times comes in the form of your being transparent with others by disclosing the truth about your life today. Where are you at today with your life? Transparency is the key to staying present and in the now—which, I think, is the only true reality and the only place where God hangs out.

CHAPTER NINE

Getting Right with the World

*"One can rectify the mistakes made in the past with
the help of fearlessness and patience."*

—The Rig Veda

Before we launch into the topic of "making right our wrongs," let's
review the spiritual tasks you've completed thus far. It is important to
reflect on the growth you've experienced since beginning this process, as it
will give you renewed motivation to continue. You need that motivation—
perseverance is critical. Indeed, your work must continue throughout your
life. Sorry if this is difficult to hear, but to succeed you have to embrace the
reality that you never fully "arrive."

When you recall what things were like before you had a mentor, before
you were part of a community, before the practice of spiritual principles
was a part of your daily routine, you'll discover that you have a different
perspective on your life and problems now. Hopefully you are starting to

experience positive results from your new way of living. Remember that one by-product of this approach to life is an enhanced sense of connection and hope. If you're not feeling it yet, hang in there. As we say in recovery, don't give up before the miracle.

Let's recap the process up to this point: First you needed to identify your problems and gather the self-honesty to realize that you lacked the power to conquer them without outside help. As a result, you became willing to change, accepting the reality of your life, and open to being taught. Maybe you were one of the lucky ones who received the gift of desperation. Maybe it was just a quiet resignation to the truth that made its way slowly from your head to your heart. It doesn't matter what gets you on the path; the point is that you get on the path. And a part of getting on the path is engaging the principles presented in this book.

You opened your mind, and possibly your heart, to spiritual concepts after recognizing some of your cognitive distortions. There was a sense of hope that started to develop when you began earnestly seeking. By now you desired change enough that you were willing to surrender the false attempts at controlling your life and those around you. Surrendering to God is probably the most intelligent thing you will ever do. C. S. Lewis captured this well when he observed that most people settle for making mud pies in the slums and give up a vacation at the beach because they are unaware of the possibility. We don't realize that ultimately our Creator only wants the very best for us—not what's boring or insipid. As we know, the good is the enemy of the great.

At some point (hopefully early on) you became part of a community where you experienced hope and acceptance at a deeper level—even while still experiencing a lot of insecurity at times. On this journey you often take two steps forward and one step back. But you pushed forward and got a mentor. That takes courage and humility. Taking direction from someone other than your brain (which is out to mug you) is difficult.

Then you took the time and the effort to write your inventories (on your resentments, your fears, your sexual relationships, your secrets, and your assets), which revealed the nature of some of your most glaring shortcomings. While the inventory process can be painful, it is also where you begin to see that God does not make junk and that there is plenty of good in you, too.

You took a huge step into cultivating a life of transparency when you disclosed your inventories to your mentor, trusted friend, or qualified religious person. The life of the imposter is now dying because you are no longer feeding it. Instead, you are feeding the force of integrity. You are in the process of getting right with your self.

Your inventories made it clear that there are many aspects to your character that are destroying your chances for true love, serenity, peace, happiness, and usefulness. You cannot wish these traits away. In fact, they will always be with you to some extent. But as you grow spiritually, you'll begin to realize that the times when you gain relief from your personality defects are God's victory, not yours. And as a result you start to grow in sincere gratitude for the changes that are taking place within you.

It now becomes essential that you live your life by taking the next right action instead of trying to think your way through things. We now begin the process of growing up emotionally and spiritually. You may think, "Why do I need to continue, especially if I'm feeling okay?" It is because in order to feel truly free and clean, you need to make sure that you're right with the people who have been harmed by your actions and shortcomings.

Maybe you have harmed yourself far more than you have harmed anybody else. You are not going to be asked to make restitution for anything that you have not done directly, or indirectly, to others. Even though this is about making amends to those you have harmed, it is really about your inner freedom. You need to have a clean Spirit in order to walk free wherever you go, and more important, to feel free inside of yourself.

Some of the people to whom you need to make restitution were listed on your resentment inventory. However, there are others—people you have no resentment toward—whom you recognize you have hurt. My friend, for instance, needed to make amends to her daughter because she had used the girl as a friend, rather than appropriately parenting her during her high-school years. My friend's husband was an alcoholic and she'd felt increasingly isolated, so she confided in their daughter instead of reaching out for more appropriate help. She eventually got into an Al-Anon program, where she undertook the twelve-step process and realized that she needed to amend her relationship with her daughter.

Interestingly, my friend's husband eventually entered recovery himself through a twelve-step program, and at the appropriate time, he made his amends both to her and their daughter. When all the amends were made, she agreed with him that in the future they would both continue to move forward. They enjoyed several happy and loving years together before he passed on.

It is so important that we do everything we can to get right with each other. We don't know how long any of us has on this planet, including ourselves. One of the guys I mentor had a long-standing resentment against his brother over a financial matter. I suggested he make an appointment with his brother for lunch. He needed to reach out and admit that he had not been a good brother to him. The brother was very grateful because (as it turned out) he was dying. It is so wonderful to see twenty years of hardened, prideful feelings practically vanish over an hourlong lunch. This happened because one person was willing to put his pride aside in order to move ahead with his spiritual program.

I also know of situations where the opposite happened. How tragic and unnecessary. I have a good friend who had an actively alcoholic dad during his entire childhood. The dad stopped drinking when my friend was an adult and has been abstinent for many years now. But sincere amends were never made and this has left a partial hole in my friend's heart. My friend's father was verbally and physically abusive. There are so many people who receive a gift like recovery and squander it because they think, "Not picking up (or mere abstinence) is the measure of successful recovery." His father does not realize that he was a wounded man who chose alcohol to medicate himself, to avoid reality, or to fill the void within. Take away the alcohol and all you have left is the same person, just not drinking. Unless the person is willing to work through a spiritual process, which definitely includes making restitution for harms done, the person is not experiencing healthy recovery.

Getting right with the world takes willingness and humility: the willingness to act and the humility to take guidance from a mentor. When I first got into recovery in the early 1990s, I went on an amends binge without any guidance from someone clearheaded and emotionally detached from the various situations and people involved. I had tons of pent-up guilt and shame that I selfishly wanted to alleviate. I was incapable of true sorrow, empathy, and compassion for the people I'd harmed during the years of debauchery.

After I read about the amends process, I went to the people whom I had harmed in some way and basically said, "I'm sorry"—a line I had used many, many times to get out of trouble. Yes, I was sorry. But there's more to making amends than that. Making restitution for harms done to another entails saying that we were wrong and articulating how we think we harmed the other person. We admit our wrongs and ask the person if we have omitted anything and listen (without defense) to their reply. Then we ask what we can do to make it right. For instance, if you owe money, then obviously you will show up with at least some of the funds owed. Sometimes, of course, the debt is far less tangible than a sum of money.

Your mentor, especially if he or she has applied these spiritual principles, will listen to why you think you have harmed somebody and then help you with what you need to say. There will be times when you need to wait, or make no direct restitution at all. For instance, in the majority of cases, you should not go to an ex-girlfriend or ex-boyfriend. The complexity of such situations makes this a tricky area, and you should ask your mentor/sponsor for advice if you have questions about this one. You are really not in the best position to determine if another person could be further hurt by your efforts. Check with your sponsor/mentor; examine your own motives and follow your mentor's advice. Your job is to be willing to go the distance in order to solidify your new life.

Recently, a doctor I mentor explained to me that he wanted to make amends to his wife. I listened, and then demonstrated to him how his excuses, rationalizations, and facial expressions would have been perceived. If he had listened to his own advice instead of seeking help, he might have sent her through the roof with anger, possibly putting an end to what was already a very strained marriage. I told him to get rid of any excuses and to stop minimizing his actions. He acknowledged that he understood. It was difficult for his inflated ego to receive this advice, but he followed the directions and got very positive results. His wife became willing to work on reconciling their marriage. It will be a while before she'll let him back into the house—and even longer before she'll let him back into her heart—but it is a journey worth the cost and the effort.

Sometimes your mentor will have you make restitution in the form of "living amends," which means that you live a certain way in order to build trust and show that you have changed. Calling your family each week, showing up at events and participating, and trying to give rather than take could be your amends to your family of origin. People are much more impressed by our actions than our words, especially when we continue to act well over time. I like the quote attributed to St. Francis of Assisi, "Preach the gospel always. In the last resort, use words." The saying is true: "Who you are speaks so loudly that I cannot hear what you are saying."

My mentor, Chuck, got divorced when his kids were in high school—a very hard blow to them, not least because the reason was infidelity. There was a long period of estrangement from his children whom he loved so much. After going through the work of amends, he now has restored good relations with two of his three children. He reaches out and makes strong efforts to be with them even though they are busy and two of them live in a different state.

When you make these amends you need to speak with sincerity and honesty, never expecting a certain outcome or response. Don't expect the other person or institution to admit their faults as well. This is your spiritual work, not anyone else's. There has to be a lot of prayer during this part of the process, as otherwise your intellect or your emotions may interfere.

The last time I made restitution was in 2007, because I had decided to go through this process several times. I completely submitted myself to the task and was willing to do whatever my mentor Chuck thought was right. In the past I had always avoided what I thought of as minor amends, like amends for gossiping. I hated to admit it, but I had bad-mouthed various people, including a few men from my intimacy group. Chuck told me that I needed to make restitution for these types of transgressions, too. I needed to admit my wrongs. I felt really uncomfortable telling somebody something they did not know, thinking it would do more harm than good for both parties concerned—especially me. Ironically, the admissions were well received, and after several years of attending this particular group, I finally felt as though I totally belonged. I even had to make amends to my boss for disparaging him, which terrified me. In hindsight, I think he gained some respect for me as a result of my honesty, and it allowed me to overcome some serious resentment against him.

If you have been the victim of abuse, you may include yourself on your amends list. You need to be compassionate with yourself. Maybe you stayed in an abusive relationship for too long and your kids got hurt as a result. Understand that you were spiritually unhealthy and that you did not believe you were worthy of anything better, or that you would be able to provide sufficiently on your own. You were living in fear. It is time to be kind to yourself and know that you have always done the best you could—given the circumstances and your state of mind. Knowing better intellectually does not suffice. You needed to experience everything you experienced to finally be willing to fully heal and take positive action.

Every time you complete an internal or external task, there is a tangible reward. In fact, dedicating yourself to this way of life is really an act of enlightened self-interest.

As an example of this enlightened self-interest, a man I mentor comes to mind. He is a person many would envy: He is one of the top amateur athletes in his sport and he owns his own successful company. He is personable, good-looking, and intelligent but tortured by the need for more of whatever he happens to be obsessed with. His addiction manifested itself in several ways, including an obsession with pornography. Since he has been in recovery and completed the spiritual tasks discussed in this book, he has experienced freedom from his obsessions.

Several years ago he lost a ton of money when he attempted to expand his business. He almost lost everything. Thankfully, he still had his family, including his two little children, who had come along after he entered recovery. He was desperately searching for answers and peace of mind. We started working through his amends-making process but he was reluctant to tell his wife about his struggles. He knew she would hold him accountable if he blew the whistle on himself. I told him that I could not take him through this process unless he first got honest with his wife.

As much as he wanted help, it still took him two months to tell her. He just said to her that he was attending a program for his addiction. Later during the amends process he was able to tell her about the pornography, which was the scariest thing he had ever done. His wife was shocked but knew that there had to have been a reason for the disconnect she had been feeling in the intimacy department. It proved to be the beginning of transparency and vulnerability in their relationship, which are essential elements of true intimacy.

Recently, he has done really well financially and he started to obsess over money again. Instead of working longer hours and lusting for more wealth, however, he gave a big check to his church in order to break his obsession. He knew he needed to make God his God, rather than some substitute god who lures with a false sense of security. It wouldn't have mattered whether he gave the money to some stranger on the street or to a well-known worthy cause. What mattered is that he was practicing spiritual principles in a tangible way. He felt great about it.

After he did this, he got a call from one of his best friends, who happened to be the CFO of a Fortune 100 company. The CFO was obviously quite rattled as he shared the news of a friend who had just committed suicide. The man who committed suicide owned a successful commercial real estate company that was struggling. The man I mentor was able to share his own experiences and struggles with money, work, power, ego, and prestige. He was able to share his recent obsession and how he broke through by giving away a significant amount of money. God uses our struggles to help others, once we surrender them to Him.

Making Amends Is a Spiritual Necessity

There are spiritual laws in the universe that are just as certain as physical laws. For example, to the extent that you judge to that same extent you will be judged. In the twelve-step world we say, "Anytime you are pointing your figure at someone else, notice that there are three more fingers pointing back at yourself." If you choose to ignore spiritual laws it does not make you less of a person. But, without even knowing it, you might be denying yourself the very things your heart most deeply desires.

Don't miss out on those things—the process works, and will take you where you want to go. Continue to push forward until you know "a new freedom and a new happiness," as promised in the recovery literature. Don't give up. This is when your hard work really pays off. If you knew what rewards await you, you would be willing to go to any lengths for a genuine spiritual experience. You do not need to act out your old patterns; you have choices now because you are not interacting with life in a mechanical fashion anymore. You are free to go wherever you want and feel comfortable going there. You have a purpose.

I am amazed at what a marvelous way of life this is, especially when I compare it to the season of my recovery when I hadn't yet tasted true freedom. I recall, for instance, having a strong fear of visiting my family whenever I returned to New York. I would get a gnawing sensation in the bottom of my stomach, wondering who I might run into from my old days of dissipation. But once I had made amends, including restitution for all the harms I'd done, I no longer had those feelings. Instead, I got excited for all that came with a trip to New York—visiting family and old friends, catching a Broadway show, going to a few recovery meetings, enjoying really good food.

In the end, you won't regret your past. Your past is what brought you to where you are today, and the shame, guilt, and regrets you hold because of it can be put into perspective. You would never have picked up this book and attempted the tasks it lays out if it weren't for your past. Ironically, your past failures indirectly led you to God. What could be more important than that?

As you make amends, you will begin to experience serenity. While adrenaline, fear, depression, anger, and excitement used to dominate your days, now you tap into the priceless gift of serenity. You will have peace because you won't want to be anywhere other than where you are. Living in the present becomes a way of life.

Your greatest gift to others will be your redeemed past and your newfound authenticity. You will feel great about being part of the solution to humanity's problems in the world. You will realize that you can be a contributor rather than a taker, because many of us were takers even when we looked like givers.

As you come to see the ways in which you are a blessing to others, you will find purpose and acceptance, regardless of the place from which you started your recovery journey. You will see how unhelpful self-pity can be and—rather than wallowing in a problem—you won't be able to tolerate being too far from a solution.

The prayer of St. Francis says, "In dying we are born to eternal life." As the unhealthy parts of our egos die, we get glimpses of this truth. We are now able to live for a higher cause than ourselves.

There is no need to be so concerned about how others perceive you when you feel secure within yourself. What a gift it is not to need to look good anymore. What a beautiful by-product of this work.

As the way you perceive life changes, your entire attitude will be different. This will not be a conscious effort. You will look at stressors as challenges to overcome through the application of spiritual principles. You will be willing to share about these struggles openly with your trusted friends.

You will begin to live from a place deep within yourself. You will now trust your feelings. You will understand how harmful negative emotions and selfishness are in your head and in your heart. Living in this place of intuition does not deny logic, but it takes you beyond it.

God is becoming your true source of power. Sometimes it feels impossible to comprehend just how much God cares about, and wants to help with, all the little aspects of your life from which difficulties arise. The fact will become clear that God is intimately involved in the details of your life.

I was in a recovery meeting in Stuart, Florida, in March of 2012 where I listened to five minutes of a woman's story and was amazed at the love and healing in her life. I knew this group by their faces and stories because I had spent a week going to meetings there the year before. The meetings start at seven in the morning, Monday through Saturday. (When I'm on the road—for whatever reason—I like to connect to a spiritually based group.)

It was an anniversary meeting, which meant that they were honoring all the people with March milestones. The woman was celebrating five years of recovery from addiction. As she spoke, she wept with tears of pain and joy.

The tears of pain came from the incest that took place when she was a child; a wound inflicted by the male figure she should have been able to trust the most—her father. And, as if that weren't enough, there was another deep wound inflicted by someone she also should have been able to trust—an army colleague who raped her. The pain was made more acute by the fact that he had barely been punished for the crime. She'd had to see him every day for over a year. He taunted her and told other men that she was a "bad" sex partner.

Her tears of joy were due to the fact that her life had been completely transformed over a five-year period. She had finally found a group of individuals who welcomed her with open arms and truly accepted her. She talked about her love for her mentor (who was present in the room), the person she had chosen to walk with her through this process of spiritual healing. She spoke of her own growth and the self-respect that she had gained. She shared about the process of making amends to herself for the years of self-hatred and resulting poor treatment of herself. She concluded by talking about how she had forgiveness for those who had abused her. She is a remarkable woman, and her life has a message for us: If she can be healed and live in gratitude, then so can we.

Gratitude is one of the wonderful results of this process. In the extended care program I help supervise, we ask the patients to journal and write out five things they are grateful for every day. It is almost impossible to be grateful and to wallow in self-pity at the same time. If you are consciously acknowledging what is good in your life—however small—in written form, you are helping to alter your thinking by focusing on the positive. Research has clearly shown that your thoughts actually dictate your feelings. When you think negative thoughts (cognitive distortions) you will eventually feel worse, and some people will end up being depressed. We will talk more about living a life of gratitude in the chapter that explores the idea of service.

Whether you have three people on your amends list or 300, it will be important to pray for willingness before attempting to make amends to them. Get the guidance needed for this essential task, then put this book down for a few weeks and attempt to make things right with a few people or institutions. Pray. Don't do this alone—follow the guidance of those who have gone before you.

CHAPTER TEN

Growing Up

*"Lord, grant that I might not so much seek to be
loved as to love."*

—St. Francis of Assisi

Consider the wisdom of this statement I heard someone make at a twelve-step meeting in New York years ago: "Don't let the good things God has given you take you away from God."

As you have gone through this process of spiritual recovery so far, your initial problems have been put into perspective. By living this way of life, you are now "in the right place at the right time." I call it "being on the Beam." Now don't start thinking that everything is fixed and that you no longer need to grow and change. Don't start moving away from the very process that changed your life just because things are getting better. Over time, you will receive the relationships and the lifestyle that fulfills you. But it will take time. You will discover your passion and mission. Don't let these dreams of yours take you away from the basics. I can't tell you how many people I have seen drift away from this beautiful way of life. It usually happens slowly and many people don't notice it—especially the ones who are headed for trouble.

We are now going to look more deeply into how we can sustain personal, emotional, and spiritual growth. You got right with God, with yourself, and with others; now it is important that you continue to grow toward your true self. This takes effort. In fact, growing spiritually can be like being on a downward escalator when you want to go up—you need to constantly trudge against the escalators. If you stand still, you will actually be going down. That is not to say that we don't take breaks in our lives. In fact, rest and relaxation are extremely important and it can be good to be intentional about recreation and spending idle time with yourself.

Growing spiritually means learning to incorporate certain spiritual principles into your daily life. You either just completed or are in the midst of the amends process, in which the focus was on past actions where you caused others hurt. Now you need to learn how to admit—as soon as an offense occurs—that you were wrong, rather than letting hurt and resentments fester and grow. Twelve step literature tells us to be aware of fear, anger, and any forms of self-hared or self-obsession. We need to ask God for relief as soon as we notice these negative thoughts or emotions. Then we need to strive to "get out of self" by being of service to others.

Cleaning up your messes as you go along is far better then letting things get messier and then straining to do a binge cleanup. The question is not, "*If* I screw up, what do I do?" The correct question is, "*When* I screw up, what do I do?" Your spiritual health, which is the most important dimension of your life, hinges on staying clean within. Think about it—it's when you are in good spiritual condition that you want to take care of yourself physically and emotionally. If we can keep our priorities straight, then no matter what happens to us in life we can feel a sense of peace. In a well-prioritized life, our right choices will be confirmed by what we eat, by how we sleep, by whom we surround ourselves with, by how much time we spend with our spouses and kids, by our quality of work, and ultimately by how much we try to connect with God.

As you grow spiritually, you learn how to accept responsibility for your part in any given situation. Learning how to say "I was wrong" will be extremely helpful in your quest for spiritual connection. Pride and fear will always be willing and able to deter you from this ego-deflating process. The question is, do you want to be right or do you want to have peace of mind? Even if you are right, if you fight to the death about it, it only shows you are still wrong. Bring your hurts and issues to your spiritual guide, to your spiritual group, and to God. Be willing to look at your part. Ask for guidance on how to deal with each situation. Please learn now that you need to honestly examine your part: own it, accept it, admit it, amend it, and get over it. Eventually, it will become part of your lifestyle and you will ask, "What would my God have me do in this situation?"

As you trust that your Creator is taking care of you, it is time to start asking how you can best serve others. That is, serve in a healthy, non-manipulative way. "How can I best show love to others?" is a much better question to ask than, "How can others best love and appreciate me?" When you are willing to dedicate yourself to the task of emotional maturity, positive results will follow. Best of all, you won't struggle against the issues you cataloged in your initial problem list. If you are going to be free from your compulsions, the key is to stay in "fit spiritual condition." You may stop your behavior, such as drinking, drugging, viewing Internet porn, binge-eating, or spending too much money, but you still won't find true relief until you practice spiritual principles consistently.

A good indication of where I am at spiritually is how I handle traffic, how I communicate with my wife, and how I feel about my supervisor at work. I can be amazingly nice to everyone outside of my little world, but my true colors come out with those closest to me. Is it so with you?

The Bible says that a wise man admonished us with the following words we need to heed:

> "Do any of you think you are religious [spiritual]? If you do
> not control your tongue, your religion is worthless. What God
> the father considers to be pure and genuine religion is this: to

take care of orphans and widows in their suffering and to keep oneself from being corrupted by the world." (James 1:26)

To me, "control my tongue" is a nice way of saying, "keep my mouth shut." And when I do mess up, it is important to open my mouth to make amends as soon as I am capable—to "get over myself." After that, I immediately try to be of service to someone.

A few years ago, a good friend of mine committed suicide. Paul was physically healthy and had everything to live for—a life many would envy. His tremendously successful career had allowed him to retire in his forties. He spent his free time in the outdoors. He was an avid outdoorsman, taking months-long fishing and hunting trips into the extreme Canadian wilderness where he would see more grizzly bears than humans.

When Paul was in Colorado we would have lunch together and share about our struggles and spiritual journeys. We really enjoyed and admired each other. He gave my son a fly-fishing lesson and I imagined the three of us on all sorts of future adventures. He had a beautiful spirit, and, like me, he had the gift of gab. And then, in a moment of insanity, a combination of factors led him to take his own life.

After the initial shock and grief over his premature death, I experienced three months of almost total reprieve from knee-jerk reactions to how others (particularly my wife) treated me—regardless of whether I perceived the treatment as good or bad. I was given an incredible ability to pause before reacting to anything. I completely understood that how I was feeling was something occurring inside of me, and that nobody had the power to make me feel anything or make me act a certain way. I understood the way Bill Wilson expressed this simple spiritual axiom: "When I am disturbed there is something wrong with me." I was able to respond rather than react to life's circumstances. I thought I had been pretty good at this kind of stuff but I learned during this period that I had still been letting an immature little boy inside of me run my life.

It became crystal clear that my biggest priority was to stay connected with God on a daily basis. The only thing that should matter was how I felt about me and how my God felt about me. Throughout this phase of increasing self-awareness, I was tapping into some serious stuff. If Paul were here, I would kiss him on the forehead and tell him that he was an amazing guy and that God adored him. I would hug him and ask him to live with my family and me until he could trust himself.

During that time, I listened to a talk by a noted psychiatrist about emotional maturity. The thrust of his message was that we need to continually heal and grow up. The speaker referred to a letter that Bill Wilson wrote to a depressed friend to illustrate his point. In one of the opening lines, the letter says, "Those adolescent urges that so many of us have for top approval, perfect security, and perfect romance, urges quite appropriate to age seventeen, prove to be an impossible way of life when we are at age forty-seven and fifty-seven."

Wilson goes on to talk about growing up emotionally, saying that after lots of prayer, spiritual guidance, and good therapy he learned that his biggest problem was his dependence on other people and circumstances to provide him with emotional security and self-esteem. When people did as he wished and things worked out, he was up. When people resisted him or his plans failed, he got depressed.

Wilson writes further about not being able to experience the prayer of St. Francis as a reality until he overcame his addiction to the world. Like Bill Wilson, we would do well to contemplate this classic expression of self- and God-awareness—and see both the struggle it implies and the ideal it holds before us.

The Prayer of St. Francis
> Lord, make me a channel of thy peace.
> That where there is hatred I may bring love,
> That where there is wrong, I may bring the spirit of forgiveness,
> That where there is discord, I may bring harmony,

That where there is error I may bring truth,
That where there is doubt I may bring faith,
That where there is despair I may bring hope,
That where there are shadows I may bring light,
That where there is sadness I may bring joy.
Lord, grant that I may seek rather to comfort than to be
comforted,
To understand than to be understood,
To love than to be loved.
For it is by forgetting self that one finds.
It is by forgiving that one is forgiven,
It is by dying that one awakens to eternal life.
Amen.

Once we go through the grueling process of detoxifying from the world, we become free to love without conditions—which is the ultimate goal of our souls.

The point is that we cannot completely connect with God until we are willing and able to love His children as He does. When we are plagued by dependency on others, we cannot really love them because there is always an invisible hook that we need them to bite on. Someone who is spiritually healthy can love you exactly the same way regardless of how you are feeling or acting toward him or her. I am now able to see how addicted I am to this world, but I am always grateful to God for showing me the truth about myself—eventually!

I got so excited about this message of emotional maturity that I couldn't stop thinking about it. A year earlier, I had done a lot of therapy regarding core issues, and here I was being presented with the next step I needed to take. I brought this message to a retreat I was co-facilitating and it was well received. Then I addressed the same subject at a workshop with a large group of people in recovery.

Afterward, I made the mistake of looking at about fifty of the seventy post-workshop satisfaction surveys. Many were quite positive, but there were a handful of negative comments. I got a little angry. When I got home, my wife asked how my talk went and she noticed that I was feeling down. She proceeded to give me a mini-speech about how at some point in my life I needed to grow up, that I needed to care only about what God and I thought about me rather than what everyone else did. She told me I needed to find contentment in knowing that I was trying to love and help people.

Then she asked what the talk was about. I said, "Not caring what others think but only what God and I think, and finding peace within from truly loving others regardless of how they treat you." She walked away shaking her head. Yes, spiritual growth is about progress, not perfection.

You'll find that after you've experienced the grace with which to overcome your biggest problems, life will ask you to expand your spiritual horizons and offer lots of opportunity to grow through more mundane daily struggles. Ironically, what we really need most of the time is a healthy dose of ego-deflation and God-inflation.

I've paraphrased the signs of emotional maturity below. What do your immediate internal reactions tell you about your place of growth as you read them?

- When you are wrong, you admit it, whether or not your partner responds in kind.
- You stop taking your partner's reactions to you personally.
- You own your own projections as an act of integrity.
- You confront yourself for the sake of your own integrity.
- Rather than pressuring others to change, you realize you must change, yourself.
- You don't demand that others listen to you; listening to yourself is sufficient.
- Validation comes from within yourself; you no longer manipulate others to get them to validate you.
- You are your own emotional supporter, instead of expecting other people to support you.

- You accept yourself as you are, instead of demanding that other people accept you the way you are.
- From your emotional reactions, you discern the unresolved issues in your life and you begin to work on resolving them.

You are attempting to implement these principles and tasks into your life as an act of self-respect. The result will be an increased sense of well-being.

You—and I and everyone else—need to constantly grow, or we will experience regression. I have never met anyone who was not at least somewhat concerned with what others think of him or her, or with trying to fulfill some recipe for success that someone else (e.g., our culture) dictated to him or her. Our goal is to be free to truly love God, ourselves, and others. Many of God's kids—His kids meaning everyone on the planet—will benefit from our growth.

Relationships

Many of us know what we need and want, which is to have loving relationships. But most of us still act out of our wounding, lashing out at those around us in a way that is far from loving. When things aren't going our way, don't we think that things would get better if only the other guy behaved differently? Isn't that why we get divorced, change jobs, switch churches, or change the bar where we hang out? The underlying belief is that in order for us to get our needs met, the world and its people need to change. However, this is just not true. It is our own perspective that needs changing.

In the addiction world we warn people in early recovery not to make major changes until they have completed the spiritual tasks offered in this book. I have heard it said many times, "We don't have relationships in early recovery, we take hostages." We "take hostages" because we do not know what we ourselves have to offer, much less who is right for us. You need to be whole inside yourself before you have anything to offer another. Love takes a tremendous amount of self-sacrifice, so you need a self to sacrifice.

You need to have a transformative experience before you can know with clarity whether you should be in or out of a particular marriage or other committed relationship. Unless the relationship is dangerous to you or your children in some form, it is worth the investment of time and patience to slow things down and undergo whatever necessary healing is called for. You are going to learn the lessons with somebody, so in most cases is best to do it with the one you are already committed to. Many times it is in the difficulty of committed relationships that we have the most pain and consequently the most potential for spiritual growth. Keep remembering that pain is inevitable, but misery is optional.

I am all about love and happiness, but the drug of a new relationship is not the way to get there. In fact, what we call "falling in love" has very little to do with actual love. Real love wants what is best for the other person, for him or her to grow toward his or her highest and best state of being. Infatuation wants the "love object" to remain exactly the same, forever. This is not indicative of a genuine interest in fostering growth—either one's own or that of the other person involved.

I believe that to love another person is as close as we can come to Godliness. God does not have a crush on us. God is not ga-ga over, crazy about, infatuated with, or addicted to us. God *loves* us—exactly as we are at this very moment—and He loves us as we will develop and grow to be, forever.

Do not live your life having society define things for you. I myself was hopelessly deluded in my twenties and early thirties about intimate relationships. I thought the "falling in love" experience would be like a romantic comedy starring Meg Ryan. The problem is that, in reality, the work of love begins exactly when the movie ends.

It is deep within your heart where you will find the greatest adventure of all time. Learning how to love those closest to you in the physical, emotional, and spiritual sense is the greatest challenge and journey life gives us.

Mother Theresa said in countless interviews that the United States suffered from the greatest spiritual poverty she had ever witnessed, and she ranked spiritual health before physical and monetary health in order of priority. She would instruct people to learn how to love their neighbors and their families before going out to save the world. Indeed, we need to learn to love those people who hurt us and judge us and know all of our weaknesses. We need to learn how to detach and let others experience their walk with God without trying to "play God" in their lives—as if we could ever really know what is best for someone else. My life clearly shows that I've not known what was best for my own growth, let alone somebody else's.

There is a story of an old farmer who had worked his crops for many years. One day his horse ran away. Upon hearing the news, his neighbors came to visit. "Such bad luck," they said sympathetically. "Maybe," the farmer replied. The next morning the horse returned, bringing with it three other wild horses. "How wonderful," the neighbors exclaimed. "Maybe," replied the old man. The following day, his son tried to ride one of the untamed horses, was thrown, and broke his leg. The neighbors again came to offer their sympathy on his misfortune. "How unfortunate," they exclaimed. "Maybe," answered the farmer. The day after, military officials came to the village to draft young men into the army. Seeing that the son's leg was broken, they passed him by. The neighbors congratulated the farmer on how well things had turned out, "how lucky you are," they declared. "Maybe," said the farmer.

You get the point.

Addicted people like me have problems with true intimacy. As one of the founders of the addiction recovery movement put it in the book, *Twelve Steps and Twelve Traditions*:

> "The primary fact that we fail to recognize is our total inability to form a true partnership with another human being. Our egomania digs two disastrous pitfalls. Either we insist upon dominating the people we know, or we depend upon them far too much. If we lean too heavily on people, they will sooner or later fail us, for they are human, too, and cannot possibly

meet our incessant demands. In this way our insecurity grows and festers."

Where relationships are concerned, my work and my marriage are the two most difficult aspects of my life. They are also the most rewarding. In the early 2000s my wife and I were constantly fighting. We had a really hard time negotiating control issues and communicating effectively. Thankfully, we attended a marriage conference where the facilitator gave some very helpful advice on how to break what he described as the "crazy cycle." The points he made are beneficial to anyone in a relationship.

The facilitator's foundational idea was that a man's deepest desire is to be respected. He wants to be the hero. He wants his loved ones to be proud of him. A woman's deepest desire is to be loved and cherished. She craves tender security. The crazy cycle is pretty simple: When a man feels as though "he gets no respect," he withholds love, and when a woman feels unloved, she withholds respect.

The concept and cycle are easy to understand; what's not so easy is to stop the cycle. As usual, knowledge can only get us so far in life. Usually, like adolescents, we think *If they would not act that way then I wouldn't need to act this way*. We become manipulative people who try to get the other person to change by punishing them with arguments, self-pity, the silent treatment, and criticism. Or we may we bottle everything up inside or act out with an affair. No wonder our society's divorce rate is over 50 percent. We desperately need help from God and each other to grow up.

So what is the answer to this craziness? A friend told me that when his mentor knows he is about to ask him a question, he says, "God is the answer, now what is your question?" How does that play out when communicating with your partner? In the heat of an argument when your feelings are getting hurt, your lover or spouse seems more like an enemy than the love of your life, right? The answer is your relationship with God.

When your relationship with God means more than anything in your life, you become willing to do anything to preserve its integrity. Your spouse can be unfairly critical and you can—with God's grace—hold your tongue, state how you feel, set a boundary, show her or him love, listen, and deal with the hurt appropriately. This not only keeps the channel of connection open to God, but it also creates an opportunity to work through the issue. If your spouse feels loved even when he or she is being unreasonable, it provides the best conditions for a positive outcome. Heck, he or she may even look at him- or herself and realize that he or she is being rude and hurtful. When you retaliate and act from your emotions, it only fuels the dysfunction. You are demanding that the other person change before you do.

Do whatever you can to improve your relationships. Don't ever stop learning and growing. There are many good books you can read and techniques you can practice, but the truth is that no book or technique is going to be a panacea when it comes to relationships. The key is to look for what God is saying to you in these relationships and to always be willing to look at yourself first.

When it comes to intimate relationships it is important to learn what it is that makes the other person feel loved. We seem willing to do very loving things during the initial phases of a relationship, but those can fade away over time and so may the warm and fuzzy feelings. That's when the work phase of the relationship begins, and along with it, the phase of *real* love.

Although we are all alike in our need for love, different people have different kinds of needs and preferred ways to have them met. For some, love is appreciated when they receive words of affirmation. For others, acts of service make them feel loved. Quality time spent with a loved one makes others feel loved. And for still others, it is receiving gifts or physical touch that creates loving feelings.

It would be good for you to figure out your partner's main needs and to act on them instead of hoping that he or she would figure out yours.

In his book, *His Needs Her Needs*, Dr. Willard F. Harley elaborates on a similar concept, which he calls the love bank. We need to keep trying to fill the bank so the other person does not consciously or unconsciously go outside the marriage to get his or her bank filled. Harley believes:

- She needs affection.
- He needs sexual fulfillment.
- She needs intimate conversation.
- He needs recreational companionship.
- She needs total honesty and openness.
- He needs to be attracted to her.
- She needs a financial plan.
- He needs solitude at times (the so-called man-cave).
- She needs him to care for the children they have together.
- He needs to be respected by her.

These are huge generalizations, and couples will have to adapt these statements to fit their respective relationships. Again, there are no true formulas, workshops, books, or anything else that will provide the complete and total answer for you. We do our part by continuing to take the necessary actions to clear away whatever gets in the way of our relationship with God. We learn to cultivate love and tolerance for others inside of our hearts. We ask God for the strength and grace to help us persist.

There is always room for improvement in our relationships. Relationships are God's gifts to us to help refine us. My hope for you and for me is that we continue to mature emotionally and spiritually. I hope that you give others around you a huge break by putting the focus on yourself for a couple of years—by that I mean to focus on what you need to change, not on what others need to change. What a huge gift it is when we can admit our wrongs, right our wrongs as we go, be of service, and treat others with love regardless of how we are being treated.

If you are finding that you cannot get beyond your behavioral patterns as you go through this spiritual process, then you might benefit from some form of trauma treatment. When we think of trauma we usually think of something like PTSD, which so many members of our military experience. But trauma comes in a wide variety of forms—many more subtle and less obvious than warfare—and can affect your thinking and behavior for decades unless it is treated effectively. I meet with traumatized individuals every day who are completely unaware of how impacted they are by certain life events or by a lack of healthy nurturing. There is plenty of information about different types of trauma therapy, such as EMDR (Eye Movement Desensitization and Reprocessing) or somatic experiencing, that you can research online or at your local library. There are some excellent therapists and trauma treatment centers that can help.

CHAPTER ELEVEN

Prayer and Meditation

"One single grateful thought raised to heaven is the most perfect prayer."

—G. E. Lessing

If you do nothing else, pray. Whether you believe in God or not—pray. Pray something like "God—if there is a God—please help me today." Whatever the area of your life in which you need help (which is every area for me), where you need insight, strength, wisdom, or power beyond your own capabilities, it will be of the utmost importance that you pray. Sometimes it is how we pray that makes the difference. For example, I often work with clients who are in legal trouble, so I tell them, "Instead of praying for outcomes like 'I pray I won't get caught,' pray for courage to walk through everything regardless of the outcome."

By now I hope that your idea of God has changed from that of a Santa Claus or critical parent to that of a loving source of power that you want to commune with as much as possible. It takes effort, like any important relationship. It takes time and commitment, but the dividend paid from this relationship will be the most fruitful of any friendships you will ever know.

Any attempt at prayer is excellent because it focuses on the intention of your heart, and it's not about how articulate or how theologically educated you are. The best prayer I ever prayed came from the bottom of my heart: "Help me!" Pray that prayer with no strings attached.

I like the notion of Big P prayer and Little P prayer, which I learned about during my spiritual direction training sessions with the Vincentian Spirituality Institute. Little P prayer is the recitation of words, prayers, conversation, talking. Big P prayer is about praying with our being, with our hearts, unity, listening, dwelling, loving. The whole purpose of Little P prayer is to lead us to Big P. Some people suggest that prayer is talking and meditation is listening—we need to do both, with an emphasis always on listening. What matters is that we attempt to stay in conscious contact with God the best we can because it is oxygen for the soul.

I tend to lose contact with the Spirit throughout the day so sometimes I set my cell phone to vibrate every thirty minutes to remind me to say, "Thy will, not mine, be done." Or to give me opportunities to just get quiet and breathe for a minute.

One thing that came out of my August 5, 1991 spiritual experience was that I became convinced that God is closer to me that my own breath. But I seem to forget that fact every day of this miraculous life. I remember a time when my sister was going through the most difficult experience of her life. Her child, Maddie, was very ill and my sister feared for her child's life. She was praying to God in total agony in her heart. She looked up and heard a voice say, "Why are you looking up? I AM right here." Extremely powerful. My niece is now in high school and she is physically healthy and happy.

I know now that God has my best interests in mind, but I didn't always know that; quite the opposite. I had always thought of God in terms of restrictions, holiness in terms of sacrifice, "lameness," boredom, and lack of passion. I could not have been further from the truth. Nothing in life could be more important than improving my relationship with God. Everything of any value rides on this process. My decision-making processes, values, capacity for intimacy, sense of purpose, peace and direction, ability to give and receive love, life priorities, the work I choose, my recovery, how I view and treat my children, how I handle my financial affairs, my perspective on my marriage—all depend on my relationship with my God. A quiet conversation in my heart all throughout the day would slow things down and help me live in the present more than anything.

That is why this relationship, which we develop through actions such as prayer and mediation, is more important than any acts of service. When my thoughts and actions of service come from me, then I am apt to take credit and catch the sickness of spiritual pride. When my actions are the result of gratitude and love of my God, then my energy is sustained and there is "fruit" from my actions because I am connected to the vine—the true power source that knows what is best. I become a channel rather than the source.

For the past twenty-two years I wake up and almost always get on my knees and ask God for help with my thinking and actions. I ask for protection from my flaws and I ask for His will to be done. In the evening it is beneficial to do some journaling and review of your day. There is an excellent book called *Sleeping with Bread* by Dennis, Sheila, and Matthew Linn that can help you develop these rituals for yourself. The book helps people ask the right questions like, "When did I feel most vital today and when did I feel most depleted?" Over time you begin to see patterns. For instance, you may notice that every time you spent more than an hour with a certain person you feel depressed. You will need to determine whether you want to keep putting yourself in that situation. Or you may recognize that you feel inspired when you hike in the woods and that you need to take the time to do more of that activity.

God speaks to us through the events, relationships, and circumstances in our lives, so we need to be aware. Where is God in this situation? What is He saying to me through it? Taking time for self-reflection can give us the ability to get the correct perspective on our current situation. We usually can't get perspective when we are in the midst of the "day-to-day," so it is important to set aside some quiet time in a special place in your home that is dedicated to prayer, meditation, and reflection.

I like to go on a couple of retreats every year to be intentional about the self-reflection process. There are plenty of good reasons to go on retreats. At a retreat I can experience fellowship, I can rest, seek God, pray, write, and meet with a spiritual guide.

Seeing and experiencing God in all things is an important part of Ignatian Spirituality, which comes from St. Ignatius Loyola and many other traditions. My hope for this part of your spiritual development is that you dedicate yourself to seeking direction and union with your Creator in all areas of your life.

A Personal Prayer Story

I first met Jack Murphy briefly in August of 1986 in a nightclub in New York. After introductions, we went our separate ways to drink illegally (at least on *my* part with a good fake ID). We met again on the first day of college at the welcoming address, and we literally spent every day of the school year together until senior year. He was my best friend for the first three years of college.

We were so close that we thought nothing of sleeping together at night—which was more like passing out together. There was no sexual attraction for either of us, but there was definitely a love between us—at least on my part. We were primarily great drinking buddies, but up to that point in my life I had never been as vulnerable with anyone as I was with him.

Jack picked up fairly quickly on how insecure I was about my capacity to thrive and about my worthiness to be a student at Boston College. Even though he studied at the School of Management and I at the School of Education, he still helped me with my papers. Mostly he helped me get things done quickly so we could go out and lose our minds. Jack became a part of my family. He came with us on family vacations and my parents and my sister loved him.

By senior year, Jack and I had started to grow apart. He began to distance himself from me because of my reputation as a reckless guy. He started hanging out with the "cool crew" of guys, division-one athletes, drinkers, money-focused, connected individuals. We graduated and I sobered up, which put me on a completely different path from Jack's. In fact, we grew so far apart that he didn't ask me to be in his wedding party (years ago he would have been my best man), nor did I ask him to be in mine. Long story short, I had pain over the demise of our friendship, because there aren't many men I can say I have truly loved.

I invited Jack to my wedding as a guest and was excited for our reunion with some old college friends in Estes Park, Colorado. I called Jack to see if he was coming in early because I wanted him to attend the rehearsal dinner and to be with my family. He returned my call with a voicemail that said, "I wouldn't miss Mike D's wedding for anything in the world." It was the last time I would ever hear his beautiful voice. Two days later he was killed in the World Trade Center attacks on 9/11.

It was a very sad, fearful, and confusing time for our nation. As it happened, Jack's memorial service was set for the same day as my wedding. Many wedding invitees who had accepted ended up cancelling their flights. After some consideration, Jill and I thought it would be better to just go through with the wedding date as planned.

In my grief I questioned how authentic my relationship with Jack had been. I wondered what his true thoughts about me were. I had anger toward the men he had been associated with before his death. I realize now that they were just lost people and prodigal sons like me. I prayed for clarity, perspective, and forgiveness. I prayed for insight, truth, and understanding.

A couple of things happened that gave me some peace that were, in fact, answers to prayer. A cousin of mine called me. This cousin had never called me in her life, nor had I ever called her. She claimed she had a vivid dream in which Jack told her something that she needed to transmit to me. It was the exact answer to my question about the authenticity of our friendship.

A couple of days before my wedding I was doing some yard work at my mother-in-law's house because the wedding reception would be held there. I was listening to music. Jack and I had had various favorite songs that we would listen to as we got ready to go out for the night. One of the songs we loved started playing and I had a strong sense that he was there, saying, "I told you I wouldn't miss Mike D's wedding for anything."

To this day, I will still hear certain Bruce Springsteen or Jimmy Buffet songs at exactly the time I need to hear them and I know Jack is telling me to be grateful for my wife and children—for life itself. Every time I hear the Beatles song "In My Life," I think of Jack.

Meditation

Meditation is the process of bringing us back to our breath, our bodies, our hearts, and our souls. It is the way to the here and now where God dwells. It is the path to silence, which has been called the language of God. It is the "listening and being" instead of the "doing" part of the spiritual world.

My sponsor Chuck told me that after he finished the Twelve Steps it became clear to him that he needed to have a meditation practice. He called a teacher and he was willing to be a student. His mentor advised me to take "sips, not gulps," even if it meant meditating for just five minutes a day. Consistency is the key to this process. He told me, "As God's kids we all have access to His power. There is no need to look outside of yourself for God."

My two favorite styles of meditation are known as centering prayer and passage meditation. Centering prayer is an ancient practice that came from unknown authors. The basic premise is that the language of God is silence and that God says, "Be Still and Know that I Am God." The "be still" refers to stillness of the mind and heart.

You take a word that has sacred meaning for you, like "Jesus," "God," "Life," "Spirit," "Love," or "Peace," and you gently repeat it when you find yourself distracted by thoughts. You need to treat thoughts as if you were window-shopping, not holding on to them in any way. The point is to practice and experience the moments when there is no attachment to any thought or emotion—when there is silence in your inner being. The practice works best when you dedicate twenty minutes twice a day to sit, breathe, and just be. You only understand how valuable meditation is when you stop doing it and find out how much balance, direction, and love it brings.

All the spiritual guides that I admire and trust speak of the value of silence in addition to other forms of prayer. For some reason silent meditation is even more powerful when it is practiced with others. Early in my recovery I would attend silent retreats directed by a mystic named Pat T. I developed friendships with people on these retreats and yet we never spoke a word to one another. Feelings would arise that I did not know were there and our task was to watch everything inside ourselves without any judgment. Ironically, more change happens during this type of practice than while trying desperately with self-will to change yourself.

The other form of meditative practice is called passage meditation. It is simple. You memorize a prayer and sit quietly for twenty minutes or up to thirty minutes if you wish and say it slowly every day, until it becomes part of your being. There are several twelve-step prayers you can use for this purpose that will have a powerful effect in your life if prayed over time through your heart. I've suggested some below.

Since I follow the twelve-step suggestion to be of service to others, I like to pray, "God, please put me in a position to be of maximum service to you and your children." I have prayed this over and over and the results have been nothing short of miraculous. If your brain resists for fear that all fun will cease when you pray in earnest, you are in for a huge surprise. I know now that God has my healing and happiness in mind and that I am the only obstacle to immense freedom and usefulness.

More Prayer Suggestions

Third Step Prayer I

"God, I offer myself to Thee—to build with me and to do with
me as Thou wilt. Relieve me of the bondage of self, that I may
better do Thy will. Take away my difficulties, that victory over
them may bear witness to those I would help of Thy Power,
Thy Love, and Thy Way of life. May I do Thy will always!"
(*Alcoholics Anonymous*, p. 63)

Third Step Prayer II

"Take my will and my life, guide me in my recovery, show me
how to live."

Prayer of St. Theresa of Avila

"Let nothing disturb you, Let nothing frighten you, All things
pass away: God never changes. Patience obtains all things. He
who has God finds he lacks nothing; God alone suffices."

I've learned that one way to connect with God is by writing letters. This
is called Epistolary Prayer. As I write to God, I express my feelings and
thoughts about any given situation. I get to make my petitions and express
my gratitude. Ultimately, I write myself into a state of surrender and of
understanding that God has always been with me and will continue to be
with me in my struggles.

I practice a form of conversation called the "gratitude game." My wife and
I play it in the car and the kids will join in from time to time. It is pretty
simple, with as many variations as you like. In the most basic form, you
express something that you are grateful for, such as your health, children,
home, struggles, challenges, and so on. When you have finished, the next
person expresses gratitude. It's hard to be in self-pity and gratitude at the
same time. Getting into gratitude is a great way to change your thoughts and
feelings, especially when you begin to truly realize that this is all a gift on
loan from God. We do not earn any of the amazing gifts we have been given.

My best days in life are when I am connected to the One. Enjoying an ice cream with my kids can turn into a wave of gratitude so powerful that I start to cry. It is just a gentle conversation with God happening throughout the day even when I am talking to someone else. God knows where you need to be and what you need to say or not say. He knows the job you will be happiest in or the home that you need to live in. He is the Source of all and HE/SHE/IT wants to commune with you and give you peace.

Letting God lead you into the mystery of His love is far better than winning the lottery or becoming a movie star. It is the treasure everyone's heart is seeking, and the majority of us do not know it.

Prayer can lead to serious interventions. A young man named Dan was in a tremendous amount of pain. He was in relapse and had decided to end his life. It was one o'clock in the morning, and Dan was alone with a gun, when the phone next to his bed rang. Glancing at the display, he recognized the number—it was a friend of his from back East. Curious, Dan answered the phone and asked his friend why he was calling him at 1:00 a.m., when they had not spoken to each other in two months. His friend said that he'd had a dream and felt he needed to see if Dan was okay.

Dan lied and said he was fine, and they chatted for twenty minutes until Dan told his friend the truth. His friend replied, "I *knew* I was supposed to call you." Dan reentered treatment and is now on his way to becoming a happy, healthy, productive citizen. Thank God his friend was also practicing the spiritual principles discussed in this book and had been able to follow his intuition. God used Dan's friend to save Dan's life.

Try not to be superstitious about all of this. It is about finding ways to open up our hearts to God and to improve our relationship with Him. Then we are able to discern more clearly what His will for us is and we feel the desire to take the necessary actions. God will use us for the good of others and the world if we seek Him first.

You will find your way once you make prayer and meditation the most important part of your day. For the next ninety days it will be crucial that you make an appointment with yourself and God for at least ten minutes every day. Use the time well, and as you feel led. My hope for you is that at the end of the ninety days, this practice will have become a part of your daily routine.

CHAPTER TWELVE

You Have to Give
It Away to Keep It

"For it is in giving that we receive, It is in pardoning that we are pardoned, And it is in dying that we are born to eternal life."

—St. Francis of Assisi

You will find as you work and apply the principles conveyed in this book that you have been given a special gift—relief from yourself. It becomes evident that the only way to keep the gift is to give it away. The spiritual world is full of paradoxes. Love is one of the only things in life that expands the more you give it away. It is time to gratefully give away your time, love, and experience. This whole spiritual process is not about you getting well and going on your merry way. It is about using the miracle of personal transformation in your life to help others.

This is a natural flow. You have moved on from being caught up inside yourself and now you have relief to a degree that allows you to be useful to others and help relieve their problems. Because you are praying, meditating, taking daily inventory, meeting with your mentor, staying involved in a spiritual community, and doing the inner work, you have placed yourself in a position to receive most of the best gifts of life. There will be an expansion in your capacity for love and healing as you live a life of service.

A marathon runner cannot stay in optimum condition without continuing to train. In fact, he or she can get out of shape fairly quickly if training stops altogether. It is the same with your spiritual health. You will find that connecting to God and being of service to others will become the actions that sustain you through all the seasons of your life.

Your relationships with other people will depend, to a certain degree, on how well you love and serve one another. There is a healthy balance between self-care and service. Others need your message of hope, change, acceptance, and deliverance from the hell and toxicity of self-centeredness. Your life message has depth and meaning and it needs to be shared in all that you do.

There is evidence that supports this whole process. In a study started in 1937, a research team selected 268 male Harvard students. The researchers studied the lives of these men over a period of seventy-two years. The Grant study, as it is called, has tracked measurable items like physical exercise, cholesterol levels, marital status, the use of alcohol, smoking, education levels, and weight, but also more subjective psychological factors such as how a person employs defense mechanisms to deal with the challenges of life. For the last forty-two years, the director has been psychiatrist George Vaillant, who came to this conclusion: "The only thing that really matters in life are your relationships to other people."

Life is about our relationships and what we have to give. There are those who suffer from the same afflictions as you and who need you—you need them, too. Remember that part of Jesus' message to his disciples was to wash their feet to model the value of service. In order to find your life you must lose it in service. "Greater love has no one than this: to lay down one's life for one's friends." (John 15:12)

You have a unique message that needs to be shared, and it is part of the ongoing healing of your wounds. Pray that God puts you in touch with people who suffer or suffered from the same life problems as yourself. Bill Wilson said something to the effect that we are not bonded together as humans because of our virtues but because of our character defects (sins, reoccurring problems, shortcoming, etc.) and our struggles to overcome them.

These principles that you are striving to live by are simply a gift from God. You would not congratulate yourself for the family you were born into because you had nothing to do with it. It is the same when you change spiritually. God gave you the tools, the people, the principles, and His power. Trying to help others is actually a formula for the greatest potential of human happiness, fulfillment, and sense of purpose. The principles are honesty, hope, surrender, courage, truth, willingness, humility, brotherly love, justice, commitment, attunement, reflection, service, and amendment. Life is all about "progress not perfection." We will never arrive; because the more we heal the more wounded we realize we are. We do not graduate until we die.

Maybe you feel as though you are in no position to help anyone, but that is a lie that our warped perceptions of ourselves tell us. Some of my friends call it the "punisher." The punisher likes to tell us that we do not measure up or gives us some version of fear-based inadequacy. Try not to buy the lie. You are a child of God and your life has a special purpose. Ask God every day to use you even though you may not even recognize it when it happens.

One of the best examples of service that I can think of is from an older couple named Dave and Carrie from Boulder. They are truly amazing people. The first time I encountered Dave was in the mid-90s when I was working as a counselor at the treatment center in Estes Park. At that time, half a world away, the Mongolian government contacted Dave because he is known worldwide as a Christian doctor and addictionologist. Apparently, Mongolia has a bad alcoholism problem and while under Russian rule the only form of treatment they knew was aversion therapy. One of the cultural norms of Mongolia is that on issues like addiction, people will only listen to medical doctors. Since Dave had a medical degree and a worldwide reputation for addiction and its treatment, he was the perfect person for the job.

I was giving a lecture on an addiction/recovery related topic and Dave walked in with several Mongolian doctors to observe. Years later, I read an article about how twelve-step recovery was started in Mongolia, and that many people were getting sober. I knew it was God working through Dave and the Mongolian doctors who carried that message to that country.

When I met Dave, I had been praying about wanting to live a more radical life, so this man who traveled the world helping people immediately intrigued me. I made an appointment to visit with him at his home. He explained that he was a missionary and that I would need to do more training with a Christian organization before I could do what he did. At the time I did not have the willingness, the finances, or the open-mindedness to become involved with a missionary organization.

Years went by, and I met and married my wife. When she and I were newlyweds, we lived in Guatemala for four months in an attempt to learn Spanish and do service work. We lived in Antigua, outside of Guatemala City. Jill volunteered in a school and I volunteered in a hospital for disabled children. We did not know what we were going to do when we returned to the US. Actually, I thought we would return to Guatemala and work in an orphanage or open one after we earned some money. I started to email Dave and he informed me that he and Carrie, his wife, would be leaving the US for a year and that my wife and I were welcome to house sit for that time. We were blessed to return to the United States to live in a great home in North Boulder, where I found work as a contract counselor and Jill found employment working with developmentally challenged kids at a high school. Through living in their house and taking care of everything I learned a lot about their lives.

Dave and Carrie have four children and many grandchildren. He was a successful physician and his employment history shows a love for people and God. Years ago he started a school to train addiction counselors throughout the world through a missionary organization. For the past few decades he has spent 90 percent of his time leading international ABC schools (Addiction Behavioral Counseling). He comes back to the US to do work in emergency rooms to support his avocation. He is over seventy-six years old and still works in full-time ministry.

His wife, Carrie, has a master's degree in counseling and she is an expert on co-dependency and trauma. They have a vast network of friends throughout the world, and I have been lucky enough to meet many of them because Carrie and Dave open their home as a training center every few years. Carrie joins Dave on most of his adventures. They seem truly happy and fulfilled. They have not become rich monetarily, although they certainly could have, but they have become amazingly blessed with connection and love of the Creator of the Universe and His children.

It is remarkable that in our society people like Dave and Carrie don't get covered in the news, but a celebrity getting married and divorced in seventy-two days does. But celebrities are not to be envied for their fame and fortune. Dave and Carrie go unnoticed but they live lives of greatness by living lives of service. They are busy training people to save lives in Africa, South Korea, Eastern Europe, Russia, and South America. They want to carry the message of healing throughout the world and they are doing a pretty great job.

While we have the intention to affect others by means of our service work, sometimes we get the most unexpected outcomes. I received one of the biggest gifts of my life through an unexpected vessel in the midst of my doing service work. Tony is a bipolar guy with some addiction issues whom my recovery group collectively mentored. One summer, he went off his medications and did some odd things. For example, he told the organizers of a young folks' conference that he would play "Amazing Grace" on the bagpipes for the finale of their presentation, although he neither knew how to play the bagpipes, nor did he own any. He had everyone hyped and he showed up as the audience was chanting his name—only to tell them the story that he ran over the bagpipes with his mother's car. Buzz kill.

It was 1999 and I was visiting Estes Park. I looked up Tony and found him to be the same basically nice, somewhat odd guy. He was off his meds at this time. He and I went to lunch at a Mexican restaurant in town, planning to get a couple of burritos. I wanted to help him.

As I was trying to convince Tony to get back on his medications and to get stabilized, out of the corner of my eye I saw the waitress approaching the table. She was an incredibly beautiful woman, with long, red, curly hair. When she came to take our order, I tried to be pleasant but struggled to conceal thoughts like, *A woman like this wouldn't want anything to do with me—just a counselor in recovery from addiction. I'm into the whole "God thing," noncontact sports, and have no money or security to offer. She's probably living with a cool guy who smokes pot, plays guitar, and goes rock climbing every weekend!* This took all of ten seconds. So I didn't interact with her. I didn't even make eye contact. I just ate my burrito and tried to talk sense into Tony.

I felt compelled to go back to that restaurant every now and then for a burrito, and within a couple of weeks a friend of mine said, "For God's sake, you're thirty-one years old—just go ask her to go on a hike with you." As I discovered, she was in between service trips to Mexico and living with her mom in the mountains (not a rock-climbing pothead guitarist) and I had intrigued her, as well. We started hiking and kayaking, having long conversations and walks, and we became good friends for a full year, without ever even holding hands. We deepened that relationship, dated, got engaged, and eventually married. After eleven years of marriage and two children, I have never been so happy.

I relate all of this to correlate back to how the gift of my beautiful wife was given to me by the fact that I took a guy, a guy who was struggling, out for lunch. Tony continues to struggle and now that I live in Denver, I get updates from a friend of mine who mentors him. I can't overemphasize how much service work brings joy into my life, and how much being there for other people has changed me for the better. And then sometimes God just throws a huge gift my way.

Just getting out of my own way, not being so self-important, and being able to take time out for other people is mysteriously rewarding. I end up in the right place at the right time when I am thinking of how I can best serve others and of what needs to be done next. No longer do I walk around feeling like I'm in the wrong place at the wrong time. It's amazing when I consider that I was led to my wife because I took Tony out to lunch. Thank God for Tony. He was the gift to *me* when I thought it was I who was doing him good. He gave me more than I could ever give him. That is usually the case when we serve, but that can't be the motive. The motive needs to be about soul survival. Your spiritual health depends upon a service-oriented mentality. You can't rely on yesterday's good deed, because you need to live a day at a time. That is where we know God exists—right here, right now—in the present.

When I worked as a contract counselor for nursing homes, a client of mine named Tim suffered from a progressive disease, MS (multiple sclerosis), and he naturally was depressed. Apparently, after the diagnosis his wife left him, taking their two daughters with her. The girls had had no further contact with him. When I learned that he had had no visitors in many years, I decided that I would be of service to him by becoming his "family."

Sometimes I would wheel him across the street to attend Mass, which was the only time he ever left the facility where he was housed. In fact, he only left his bed in his room for breakfast every morning. He watched TV all day long and he faded in and out of sleep. In the last years of his life, he could no longer communicate through words, so conversations were tough. He had seriously restricted mobility and was only able to push the "on" and "off" buttons on the TV remote. The whole scene was incredibly sad.

Of course, there were some bright spots in his situation. Some of the women who worked in his facility loved Tim and were able to understand him even though he did not speak. My wife's aunt Jane lived nearby, and she visited him a couple of times per week for several months at the end of his life. She would bring her children, Jill's cousins, and her grandchildren. When I visited Tim I got extremely grateful for my own life situation. It didn't matter how I was feeling about entering the nursing home or whether or not I wanted to be there. The wonderful thing about Tim was the fact that he always managed to smile when he received a visitor—he was always thankful for visitors.

My perspective always changed and my problems would diminish or cease to exist altogether during a visit to Tim. One of the reasons is that while trying to be there for someone else, by listening or serving in some capacity, I have a reprieve from the burden of self-centeredness. Actually, most of the time I did not want to go visit, but my Irish guilt and sense of obligation to Tim would motivate me.

I got the call that Tim was in hospice on a Thursday, so I decided to visit him to say goodbye that Friday. When I got to Tim's room, his sister was there. I listened as she told him to "fight through and live." When it was my turn to speak, I told him that he needed to try and forgive his wife for divorcing him after his MS diagnosis, but his sister stood behind me and said, "We will never forgive her!" Needless to say, that visit was not a complete success.

I went back on Saturday and brought Jill and the kids to say goodbye. During that visit, I was able to hold Tim's hands and say what was on my heart. I told him that we loved him and that he was a good man. I expressed to him in several ways that it was okay to let go. I stared into his eyes and told him that God was real and that it was time to let go, to forgive, and go home. It was an awe-inspiring moment between us.

The next morning I was in a bad mood. Jill told me to get over myself, go upstairs, and spend some time praying and meditating before my daughter got out of bed. I went out on our porch and as I was praying, a bird kept chirping behind me. It was loud! I felt as if it were going to peck me in the back of my head so I turned, stood up, and stared at the bird for a minute. It stared back at me so I waved my arm and it flew away. My phone rang; it was Jill's aunt, Jane, texting to inform me that Tim had passed away. I'd had that bird encounter within minutes of his death. My daughter thinks Tim was on his way to heaven and told the bird to let me know that he could fly and dance now.

The day after Tim's death I was listening to the radio in the car on my way
to one of my men's meetings, when I heard a song whose lyrics are about a
man dancing with his daughter at various ages—when she is a young child,
then a teenager, and then before her wedding. I began to weep sitting in
my car outside the meeting place, and I only lasted fifteen minutes in the
meeting itself. I felt compelled to go home to feed my five-year-old daughter
some oatmeal, chase her around the house as "Great Balls of Fire" played on
the stereo, and then dance with her. I told her how much I loved her, that
her hair smelled like flowers, and that I would always be happy to dance
with her. I placed her gently on the couch and she had a huge smile on her
face; so did my wife, who was looking at us from the kitchen.

Tim's death helped me see the preciousness of every moment we have
with our loved ones. I think it was super-cool that he took the time to say
goodbye to me. He gave me a lot more than I ever gave him. I guess that is
how service works.

Service could be a simple sincere prayer for somebody or a word of
encouragement to someone—anyone. It could be in the form of a project
or a trip to build a house for a needy family. My dad (a retired banker)
volunteers at the local animal shelter by doing the books for them each
month. My mother (a retired social worker) brings meals to shut-ins, helps
at the local thrift store, and is a hospice volunteer. My sister creates amazing
artwork that is auctioned to benefit the local hospital. My wife uses her
bilingual language skills to help Spanish-speaking immigrants get access to
services in our community. She befriends them, cares for them, and invites
them into our lives.

There are thousands of ways to be of service. I am blessed because I get
to merge my personal and professional interests and passions. But don't
think for a second that I am receiving any huge spiritual benefit from my
job alone. It is a paid position that I enjoy. I am considered an expert in
addiction treatment. It is a whole different story with the men that I mentor
at 6:30 a.m. before work—for free and for fun. I do it because I have been
given a gift and I need to share it or it goes away. I spend time with these

guys and take them through this process of healing because it keeps me sane, grateful, and connected to God. These men are a huge gift to me.

There are men in my groups who do not mentor anyone, but they give back by taking service positions like group treasurer, coffee maker, literature representative, greeter, etc.

In recovery we say, "Trust God, clean house, help others." Helping others could be as simple as giving them a ride to a meeting or filling someone's coffee cup—and doing it with a smile. The best is remembering somebody's name and saying hello to him or her. The ultimate is making someone feel comfortable by sharing your own story so they can identify and feel less shame because they realize there are others who "struggle with the same issues that I have." We help heal others by appropriately sharing our own wounds. We give people permission to be themselves.

When St. Francis says that in dying we awaken to eternal life, I take that literally and metaphorically. As our fear-based egos continue to try to regain control, by the grace of God, we take the action of service (death of self) and come to real life. I am the happiest I have ever been in my life with the most inner freedom I have ever experienced. But on paper I am more restricted now than I have ever been. I have full-time work, six guys I mentor, obligations to my church, two young children, my wife, recovery meetings, community group, daily exercise, weekly yoga, writing a book, leading a professionals' program, house projects, meditation practice, and more! I am fulfilled and I have been given a sense of purpose, all due to living a spiritual way of life, which requires constant practice. My road is becoming narrower but my horizons are widening.

My mother naturally thinks of others first. I do not think I will ever get there. My first thoughts each day are still about me. I need a program of action that helps me get out of my false self on a daily basis. I feel most alive when I am transmitting the message of hope and healing that these principles embody. I thank God for this way of life. I cannot think of a better deal for a guy like me.

Jesus said, "Whoever loses his life for my sake shall find it." Do you believe that some form of service to others is a huge part of the answer to your questions about your life purpose and sense of fulfillment?

Ultimately, it is not about a transformation of the world, but a transformation of yourself. Even something as short-term as our service work trip to Mexico left a profound impact on me. I came back to the States with a whole different view of poverty. I realized, among so many other things, my own and this great country's sense of entitlement.

On reflection, it was one of the simplest observations that had the most impact on me. I observed my judgment of several of the team members at the beginning of the trip and how it changed, the more information I learned about them. The more I knew about my fellow workers, the less critical I became, because I understood a little more of their backgrounds. I felt an appropriate sense of guilt from my initial prejudice. The two-month trip, living in harsh conditions, changed me.

We each have a gift to give the world. I remember going down to Mississippi to help with the Katrina tragedy. I was motivated by the powerlessness I had felt and by my inability to help those suffering after 9/11. I'd told myself that I wanted to start volunteering nationally or internationally after any catastrophic event if I were able to get the time off work.

I made enough calls and found an organization called Hands On that said I could stay with them in a church in Biloxi and help out. I thought with my counseling background I could do grief and trauma counseling. I gathered lots of Walmart gift cards to hand out and left on my journey. Long story short, I was not as helpful as I thought I could be. Basically, I helped clear out a couple of houses that were flooded that were probably eventually condemned. I felt defeated because I did not feel useful during the days I was there.

The night before I left Mississippi, I was talking with a professor from MIT who had come down there for similar reasons. She had noticed that I was not partying at night like the other relief workers were doing to alleviate their stress. Relief workers and other high-intensity/high-stress workers are notorious for acting out their secondhand trauma by drinking, drugging, and acting out sexually.

I told her about my recovery from addiction and that I was going to a twelve-step meeting across town that evening. She asked to join me and later told me that she had been abstinent for six months but that she'd planned to "fall off the wagon" that night. After the meeting she had a different perspective. She felt a renewed sense of strength to continue without relapsing back into her old destructive behaviors. Who knows, maybe I was down there for that one intervention. I felt used for the good, and maybe she has stayed on the path since and helped other people in Mississippi and at MIT. We do not get to know these things—thank goodness. Our feeble egos couldn't handle it! As I said before, in the twelve-step world, ego stands for Edging God Out.

The task for this stage of your development is to commit to a couple of hours of service work per week for six months. I hope that eventually it will become a way of life for you without ego, because—as many of the sages acknowledge—it is enlightened self-interest. Pray to be used by God even if you are unaware of it. In fact, that would be the best-case scenario, because you'll be in no danger of spiritual pride.

This leads us to our next task, which is to develop a personal mission and vision. A few of my friends and I attempt to carry the message that there is a solution for the sufferer—through the practice of spiritual principles. We stress the fatal nature of our addiction, and share with others about how we followed a spiritual path out of hell.

What is "it" for you? Are you an addict? Do you struggle with anxiety, depression, obesity, or greed? What were the struggles that made you feel enough pain to read and use this book for personal growth? Pray that God brings people into your life who struggle with the same issues as you do, so that you can reach out and share your story with them. Your story needs to reveal your struggles and the solution of living by spiritual principles. Your life only just began as you stopped living for yourself and started living for what you can contribute. Look for opportunities to serve as an act of self-preservation and out of gratitude for the life you have been given.

My ultimate Saturday is when I get a super-early quiet time with good prayer and meditation, morning twelve-step meeting, and a run before the kids wake up for the day. I cook them a big breakfast of healthy pancakes, pure maple syrup, and turkey bacon. If there isn't some sporting practice and depending on the season, we take off for Boulder or a state park. If it is Boulder then we hit the farmers' market and get fresh treats and then go on a hike in the foothills. Afterward we hit the Pearl Street mall for ice cream and Starbucks for me. If there is time when we get home we can meet up with some friends for dinner. I cherish weekends with my children. I hope you do not miss this precious time thinking there is anything more important in life than relationships. I feel as though God comes to me through experiences I have with my wife and children. I want to go out and save the world and most of the time God is telling me to love my wife and children better.

I find that whenever I am in a good place physically, emotionally, psychologically, and spiritually—in other words, whenever I have all my ducks in a row—I want to take credit for it. No wonder that every time I tell someone about how well I am doing I can almost guarantee that I am about to get slammed into the concrete pavement of life. It happens because I am speaking to the person from a place of ego, not from a place humility and gratitude.

When we speak from a place of true humility and gratitude we know that our life is a gift and that all credit is due the Creator. This attitude propels us to want to serve more because we intuitively understand that we are being taken care of and blessed. Our life of service will help sustain us during hard times. There will be hard times because we are human and this is part of the human experience.

I hope that you receive the message that you have something to give to others—whether it be your time, your money, your expertise, your prayers, or a combination thereof. The implementation is the hard part, so you need to be of service to someone *today* in order to get momentum. This week you need to pray and commit to some form of service work—and act on it. We all know intellectually what is right, but it is the practice and the living of the ideals that is the hard part.

CHAPTER THIRTEEN
Personal Mission

"Everyone has been made for some particular work, and the desire for that work has been put in every heart."

—Rumi

As I write these words, I am helping to facilitate a retreat for thirty-five individuals from many different twelve-step groups at a retreat house; with me will be my friend, Fr. Dick. There will be overeaters, sex addicts, alcoholics, codependents, and workaholics. Dick has Stage 4 lung cancer with only months to live. (He may not survive to see his story told in this book.) This is to be our last time together facilitating a retreat.

In between talks with the retreat attendees I have taken some time to myself to walk, pray, mediate, sit, breathe, and just spend some idle time. Thus, all is intentional because I am on the go most weekends with my wife and kids, with sports, birthday parties, hikes, skiing, church, etc. This is a chance for me to slow down, shut the cell phone off, and honor a friend.

The reason I am able to be here to honor my friend, to facilitate a retreat, to walk, pray, and meditate is a direct result of my getting clear about my priorities. I know what my values are: I value the importance of friendship, of cultivating a relationship with my God, and of giving back what I have been freely given. These are my high priorities and part of my life vision. What is your life vision?

If you have never even considered this question, please don't despair: an easy way to start this process is to imagine you are ninety years old and on your deathbed. Will certain people surround you? Who are they? Will it be your children, grandchildren, and good friends? How intimate are those relationships? What are you leaving behind for memories? What have you accomplished? Has your work benefited others? In what ways has your life impacted the community around you? What is your view of death? How is your relationship with God? Were your dreams fulfilled? Did you have integrity? What kind of man or woman have you become? Was your work meaningful? Did it enable others, like your children, to better themselves? Do you have regrets? Do you know love?

Ask yourself these questions as if you knew you were to die today, and from the perspective as if you had been granted many more years to live. Take this last assignment seriously. Journal as much as you need to and then simplify, because the time you take to do this exercise will enable you to see the elements of your life that are extraneous to your life vision—the elements on which you will want to stop spending time and energy. For instance, you may find yourself working less because you realize that making a little more money and impressing your boss and co-workers have no relevance in your life vision. It may result in your watching far less television, or being more intentional about the programs you do watch.

The clearer the perspective you have from that imagined deathbed scene, the more informed you will be about how to live today. In my work with recovering addicts I've observed that they have such a short-term, instant-gratification view of life that they make poor decisions, which leads to pain and unhappiness. If, as part of their recovery, they could have a life vision, they would make better choices—even if they prove to be painful in the short run—for peace, contentment, love, and connection in the long run.

There are many ways to get clarity about your values, hopes, mission, and vision. The way I designed my mission statement was a fairly simple process. I was attending a three-day seminar on work and financial disorders and one of my assignments was to go take an online character test. From that test I learned that my top positive character traits were spirituality, humor, vitality (passion), bravery, honesty, curiosity, and love.

The workshop presenter gave us about thirty cards, and we had to rank them in importance when it came to work. My top five were the following:

- Adventure: I want work that has a sense of adventure. I sometimes enjoy risk-taking.
- Time/Freedom: I want to schedule my own time and be in charge of my own time clock.
- Self-loyalty: My primary loyalty is to myself, not my workplace. Benefits and salary will motivate me.
- Family-centric: I consider my family the center of my world and my employment needs to fit around my family needs.
- Better the World: I want to know that the work I am doing will contribute to making the world a better place.

Out of that exercise I developed a relatively short mission statement. "I have been granted by God the courage to live out my spirituality with passion. I embrace the adventure of loving my family and making the world a better place. I am loyal to myself and I take advantage of the time I have been given. I live with integrity and a sense of humor."

A way to conceptualize your vision statement is to think of who you want to become and what you would want to accomplish (in a perfect world). You need to think big because it is an act of faith where God can take you. There is no room for false modesty here. We need to have an idealized direction. Your mission will describe your sense of purpose and the qualities you possess that will help you fulfill your mission. Try to embed your values and priorities into the statement.

From your personal statement you can begin to formulate a map for yourself that can include short- and long-term goals and objectives for who you want to become and what you feel led to achieve. The trick is to remain in the day, staying present, while looking toward the future and doing your part to realize your dreams. It is much more important to learn to accept and love yourself, thus I want to emphasize the human *be-ing* versus the human *do-ing* aspect of this.

I spend time each year journaling and mentally revisiting some of the important areas of my life. I acknowledge any progress I have been granted by my God in my recovery from the illness of addiction. I look at the important relationships in my life—my wife, children, biological family, extended family, male friendships, men that I mentor, men that mentor me, and other families that we spend time with. I list the books, music, movies, and documentaries that have affected me most. I write about the travels I've undertaken, with and without family. I analyze work accomplishments and continuing education. There is a focus on my level of consistency with weekly exercise, yoga, contact with nature, connection with church community, training for athletic events, meditation, step work, etc. I write about the highs and lows of the past year and I look back on my goals, hopes, and dreams to see if I am headed in the right direction. In all of it I look for the hand of God.

Then I formulate goals and objectives for the next year. It has become simpler as the years fly by. I want to grow in my capacity to love others and stay connected to God. There are a hundred minor aspects to these lists of goals and dreams, but overall they are so important for me to have a sense of true purpose.

Personally, I struggle with the desire to live spiritually and be worldly at the same time. I imagine a life like that led by the singer Bono—I really admire the guy. He seems to have no problem indulging in the comforts of this world while helping thousands, maybe millions of people with his efforts in Africa and other places. The more spiritually fit I am (which is 99.9 percent a straight-up gift) the more I can accept and embrace reality. I need to remember that.

The bottom line is that I can plan, dream, and execute, but what I really need is to leave room for the "Thy-will-not-mine-be-done" factor to override everything else in the equation. One thing that long-term recovery from addiction has given me is a deep knowledge that God knows far better than I what I need in order to be happy, joyous, and free.

I remember a funny (but not-so-funny) story one of my mentors once told me. He was divorced and had part custody of his son, living in a suburb of Denver. He wanted to meet a romantic partner while the people in his spiritual group kept advising him to pray for patience, to let go, and to ask for God's will to manifest itself in his life. He really wanted to be in an intimate relationship and eventually disregarded what others were telling him. Finally, he got sick of praying for patience and he said something like, "God, I am sick of this. I want to meet someone now—I am serious!" Minutes after he thought those thoughts and prayed those prayers, his kid asked him to go outside and play catch with a Frisbee. They went outside and encountered the next-door neighbor and her child—the neighbor was soon to be his girlfriend, and eventually his wife. But problems soon emerged. "Mike," he said to me, "since I got married, I have been praying for patience!" The marriage did not last.

It is important that you let your Higher Power into your vision process. God really does know what is best for you and me. In a world of instant gratification it may not appear as though God is interested, because things do not seem to be happening fast enough. Somehow we need to get back to practicing delayed gratification by trusting God in the process.

This is the essence of the spiritual path that I am attempting to transmit. I thought it would be my gifts and talents that needed to be shared. I thought that using these qualities would be my contribution to society, or life, if you will. It turns out that it is my sometimes-healed or semi-healed wounds that are my way to empathy, connection, and assistance to others. I have found a different way to live. I am willing to share my life and my experiences, and in so doing show you a way out, if you wish. This could be your path, too, if you so choose.

Jesus says, "Abide in me, and I in you. As the branch cannot bear fruit by itself, unless it abides in the vine, neither can you, unless you abide in me." (John 15:4) Positive things will come to you and others if you stay close to your Creator and pray for the willingness to be of service. If you have done this work then your message is clear and simple, but not easy. Your vision needs to be aligned with the grace you have received and your willingness to be used for the good of others and the good of the planet.

On the flip side, I don't believe that life is a competition about how good we can be. It is okay to desire certain comforts and experiences. In my recovery I have had many dreams come true that keep me seeking and believing. I remember one time I was talking to God while hiking by myself in Rocky Mountain National Park. I told Him that I was unsure about the afterlife or reincarnation and all "that stuff," but I did know that we have at least this life. I told Him that I wanted a life like that depicted in the movie *Indiana Jones and the Temple of Doom*. I imagined living a life where I'd be teaching in some classroom when suddenly there is a quick knock on the door and someone asks to speak with me in the hallway. The person tells me that I am needed to go on an adventure for a few weeks to help people.

So there I was (true story) as the Director of Counseling at Bishop Machebeuf High School in Denver. I was teaching a class on spirituality and running it like a treatment program. Everybody told their life stories—jocks were breaking down and crying and receiving support from the drug addicts with whom they had never spoken, because they hang in different cliques. The minority students were bonding with the white kids, because everyone was identifying with their inner feelings and perceptions rather than their outward appearances. It was truly amazing.

I got back to my office after class one day and found a message from Dan Smith, a medical doctor. He said he needed me to fly to JeJu Island off the coast of South Korea. I received permission from the school to take a short leave and said goodbye to my students. I was given an interpreter and asked to teach these incredible, eager people about addiction, recovery groups, the Twelve Steps, etc. I heard the "Indiana Jones" theme music in my head as I stepped off the plane to do my thing. It was such a great experience that I could not accept payment, so I used that money to buy recovery materials in Korean for use on the island.

There is a way to combine travel and fun with vision and service. I am not great at it but there is a way to really enjoy the whole process. I love adventure and I love my family. Most of my recent dreams and life visions entail incorporating my family into my travel adventures. What are your dreams? Get them down on paper and visualize them happening even if it sounds impractical and silly.

So take some paper right now, and start writing a hope list for each area of your life, including employment, family, friends, relationship with God, interests, health/fitness, legacy, impact on your community or society, work, travel, etc. You can have as many categories as you wish. Write down what is important to you. Who do you want to be? Who do you want to love? How do you want to be of service? It will take you a couple of hours per year even if you do the minimum, and it will still have a strong impact on your life. Many people will take the time to visualize their hopes and dreams for ten minutes per day.

Take those lists and start to narrow down the themes and start to prioritize the importance of each subcategory. Whatever your lists turn out to be, you can start to condense a lot into a life vision. Ask God for help. Ask a professional for help if you think that will be helpful. Read the *Seven Habits of Highly Effective People* or one of those business-oriented self-help books. They can help. A life coach can be very helpful during this process, too.

Think big but take the small actions today that will take you toward the manifestation of your hopes, dreams, and visions. Again, using the marriage example, it does not matter how you "feel"—give your partner a hug today because that is a small action that you can take toward a loving and healthy marriage or partnership. It is building a lifestyle around the little things— today—that will bring you toward the realization of your larger vision.

Practice the principles conveyed in the chapters of this book and they will completely transform your life. Do not let the good things that God gives you take you away from your primary relationship, which is with God. Do this, and it will provide you a way of living that is second-to-none.

> *"May the rains sweep gentle across your fields,*
> *May the sun warm the land,*
> *May every good seed you have planted bear fruit,*
> *And late summer find you standing in fields of plenty."*
> —Irish Blessing

The Gift of Fulfillment Activities

Although this book is based on the principles of twelve-step recovery, there are more than twelve activities suggested throughout the book, and reviewed in this appendix. There are several reasons why this is so.

The identification of issues and problems is broken out into several separate activities, as this book is intended for non-addicts, who may not have a clear idea of what their issues are upon beginning the process. (Most addicts have a pretty good idea, by the time they get into recovery.)

Further on in the book, the inventory procedure is explained in detail for each topic to be inventoried: Resentments, Fear, Sex, and Secrets, although the process itself is essentially the same for each. What addicts in recovery would discover and discuss in fellowship meetings and with their sponsors is here introduced and explained for non-addicts in some detail.

It is suggested that you follow the activities in order. You will do some activities once, and some more than once, some in solitude, and some with mentors or members of a group, just as members of twelve-step fellowships do.

The only materials needed are something to write in, something to write with, and the willingness to be thorough and honest.

1. Activity for Chapter One

Write about what you hope to receive from reading this book. Write about your life and what you are seeking. What do you believe are your problems? What are you willing to do to find serenity, healing, and fulfillment? Remember that you do not have to be an addict to benefit from the method of working the Twelve Steps that I describe.

2. Activity for Chapter Two

Write down whatever it is that bothers you. You would not be human if you did not have problems or challenges. What is it in your case? It will usually be something concerning a relationship, work, money, physical heath, psychological or emotional health, addiction, codependency, or spiritual crisis. In most cases, it will be a combination of factors that lead to life becoming unmanageable. As you make your list, think about what causes this to be a problem for you. (Hint: try to avoid the thinking that tells you the cause of the problem is outside of yourself).

3. Activity for Chapter Two

You cannot receive the gift of a healthy spiritual life that leads to fulfillment until you look within and get honest from your heart. What is it that you need to get honest about? What do you need to accept about your circumstances? What are the facts about your current condition? What are you using to fill the void ?

The task for this chapter is to journal about your issues:
- Review and comment on the questions in Chapter One. For example, what do you believe are your problems?
- Write about the ways in which you have tried to control your issue or problem—such as your debt, anger, relationship, eating, etc.
- For each of these, what were the outcomes?
- What are the negative consequences in each case? For example, "By working eighty-hour weeks, I've become very distant from my wife and now she wants a divorce."

- How do you feel as you get these things down on paper? Make sure that you attach a feeling word (angry, sad, hurt, happy, etc.) after each negative consequence.
- Are you ready to get help? What are you willing to do?
- Are you open to utilizing practical spiritual concepts even if they may not seem to directly address your issues?

Once we establish a certain degree of self-honesty, it leads us to the next task or phase of development. When we get honest with ourselves, it is time to get out of the problem and into the solution—immediately. You have no time to waste!

4. Activity for Chapter Three

The core of your current task is to stay open minded, especially if you have been on some either specifically religious or specifically secular path. When we are open-minded we are reachable and teachable. The question is pretty simple, "Are you willing to believe in the possibility of a Higher Power? Are you willing to believe that God (Higher Power, Creator, Spirit of the Universe) could help you with your problems and issues?" If you have a belief in God, then the question is, "Are you willing to have God or a Higher Power reveal Him- or itself to you in a different way?" For example, if you are a Christian and believe in your heart that Jesus is the only way to the Father, I am not asking you to challenge or let go of that belief, but I am asking you to allow Jesus to meet you in an entirely different way. Christ encountered the most difficulty with religious people because they tended to be convinced that they knew what or who God was supposed to be based on the scriptures. On the other hand, individuals who felt they were hopeless— tax collectors, prostitutes, and uneducated fisherman—could see what the teachers of the scriptures could not. Would you walk past Jesus if he were here today because of your current perceptions and belief system? Write about this what you currently believe and what you want to believe.

5. Activity for Chapter Three

In the rooms of recovery you will hear people say, "We came, we came to, we came to believe." Coming to believe is a process that goes deeper and deeper every year that you commit yourself to the work. One thing is for sure: there is a lot more going on than you can see around you.

Before moving forward, you need to get clear about the thoughts and actions that have consistently not worked for you. What do you keep doing over and over again while expecting a different result? Write it down. What is the common denominator in these unhappy situations? Is it you?

What are the thoughts and actions that lead you back into a negative situation and thus to an undesirable outcome? (Usually they include the idea that, "this time it's going to be different.")

6. Activity for Chapter Three
If you struggle with the whole "God idea" like many of us do, it may be helpful to look back on the coincidences in your life. Look at the random events that have unfolded and look for your God in each. Who were the people or things placed before you at certain times throughout the seasons of your life? Maybe you were introduced to a particular sport or a form of artistic expression at just the right time. Maybe someone introduced you to the world of science, the written word, or a youth group. Maybe someone believed in you when you did not believe in yourself. What we don't want to do is confuse God with religion—they are very different things. Religion can help point you toward your God, like a map can help you see your desired destination, but you can never confuse the map of a place with the actual place itself.

Take note of the "coincidences " that happen in your life and ask yourself, "are these really just coincidences?"

7. Activity for Chapter Three
For this chapter, your task is to consider and then write down your answers to the following questions.
- What do you want God to be to you if you could ask for any type of relationship?
- What are your toxic images of God? Or what have been your distorted images of a Higher Power?
- What have been your negative experiences with religion?
- Where do your religious beliefs come from? Are you willing to examine those beliefs?
- How do you view nature? And the feeling, act, or concept of love?

- Do you believe there is hope for you? If yes, why? If not, why not?
- Are you willing to give the idea of an "all-loving God" a chance?

8. Activity for Chapter Three

It starts with the question, "What can you believe right now?" and "What do you believe?" It is time to decide to surrender to, and to rely on, something greater than yourself (the God of your understanding). Getting those thoughts down on paper and sharing them with somebody is important. In the end, our understanding has to be something that we come to on our own terms.

9. Activity for Chapter Four

What are the thoughts that occupy us? "What is going to make me secure and successful? What do I want? What are my needs?" These types of conscious and unconscious thoughts can guide our lives. Do you see then how we all become self-consumed in trying to get what we want or think we need?

10. Activity for Chapter Four

There is an addiction recovery prayer that says, "God, please put me in a position where I can be of most service to You and to Your children (all peoples)."

It is time for you to write a prayer wherein you give your life over to the care and protection of God—for real. Express this prayer to someone you trust or address it directly to your God.

It is not my job to try and convince you of the existence of the Divine within you. It is your job to wrestle with those questions/truths. Be kind to yourself—especially if you have experienced past traumas. Do the best you can. I like the saying, "Easy does it, but do it." Write a prayer and say it with your heart, emphasizing the giving of your life and will over to the care of your Higher Power. Say it every day (for the rest of your life, if you need to).

11. Activity for Chapter Five

Identify between one and three groups or organizations that you will engage with over the next couple of weeks. It will be very important that you give these groups/organizations a true chance by attending the functions for at least three months before making a decision to leave (unless it is harmful or abnormally dysfunctional). Remember what they say in the rooms of recovery: "go until you want to go."

I am asking you to watch less TV and read fewer fantasy books or spend less time playing games on your computer. I am asking you to work out a deal with your neighbor or family member to watch your kids one night a week so you can attend the group. Ultimately, by taking time to care for yourself you will be a more loving parent, a more productive and positive employee. It may seem counterintuitive, but I've seen it work.

You may say you already have friends and don't need a group of this kind. But it is not enough that you have a few drinking buddies or five-hundred Facebook friends. Our souls yearn for a deeper connection with each other. Age, gender, political views, religious views, salary, and professions are not significant factors in this process. In fact it would benefit you to keep these things low on the priorities list when looking for a group to join. The things that matter are your areas of wounding and your desire for positive connection.

If you are already a member of a few spiritually nurturing communities then complete a gratitude list for each of these organizations. Focus your mental energy on what good this community has done in your life. Make a commitment to give back to it cheerfully. There is no perfect community because communities are comprised of people who are wounded. Maybe you are wounded, too, and accepting and being part of these organizations is a way for you to accept and love yourself as imperfect and in the process of becoming who you are meant to be.

If your community is sick, then ask yourself what you can do to be part of its healing and then do your part. It is much easier to judge than to take a risk. Life is short, so take the risk. Journal about it and share your thoughts and experiences with your mentor or trusted friend.

12. Activity for Chapter Six

In the twelve-step programs I belong to, we call our mentors "sponsors." In the "real world" such guides are often called "mentors." You'll notice I have used both terms in this text. If you have a spiritual mentor in your life it is advisable that you use him or her consistently. If you don't yet have one, I strongly suggest you find one. Where are you going to find your spiritual mentor? If you are a member of a religious organization then it should be a little easier than for someone who is not connected to a spiritual community. But if you followed the suggestions in earlier chapters you should already be part of a spiritual community. In this case, you could be situated to look for someone that has been down the path longer than you. He or she does not need to be older than you—just more experienced in overcoming your particular problem or more advanced at utilizing spiritual concepts. He or she could be a small group leader or someone from your spiritual study group. Often the group's pastor, rabbi, or leader may have a few people whom they can suggest. Sometimes it is actually the clergy member him- or herself.

13. Activity for Chapter Seven

Open your notebook. Begin by putting a prayer at the top of the next clean page, a prayer asking that your God will help you to see the truth. There is not a right or wrong thing to put on the resentment inventory. If a thought comes to mind, do not question it—get it down on paper. If need be, fill up a whole page with names of people who have hurt you, annoyed you, angered you, and so on.

Then think about why you are angry or hurt. What's the cause? For example, "She hurt me because she cheated on me. She went behind my back and she lied to me. She is untrustworthy." Put down on paper why you have negative feelings towards this person—or institution. Haven't you ever had resentments toward institutions like collection agencies, car dealerships, or the IRS? Write them down. Be as blunt as you can. Honesty is essential. It's not about length. Don't scratch where it doesn't itch, but pray that pride and denial will not hinder the process. You may have ten resentments or you may have one hundred and ten resentments—the number is not important.

The third part of the process of creating a resentment inventory is to figure out how that person or situation affected you. Did he or she affect your ambitions, personal relations, self-esteem, emotional security, physical security, financial security, sexual relations, or personal relations? There will be fear behind most of these "-securities." When anything threatens one of your instincts—instincts that are God-given—you may become fearful and form resentment. We all have certain instincts for love, affection, shelter, food, survival, and sex. Every human being has basic instincts. When these human instincts start to run your life, when you want more than your fair share of affection or more of your fair share of anything, relationships begin to break down.

I often hear recovering addicts say, "My drug of choice is 'more.'" When your instincts start to dominate you, you want more of whatever it is you want. It might be something as apparently benign as financial security. A typical, resentment-driven reaction might be, "If you get between me and my money, I think you're trying to rip me off." If you think that way, you will go into instant resentment mode.

Here is a very short example of what a resentment inventory could look like:

Resentment-Person or Institution	The Cause	Affects My	My Part
My Boss	Promised promotion; never came through	Self-esteem	Lied on expense reports
		Financial security	Passive-aggressive; Said yes to projects then blew them off
		Ambition/Fear	
	Criticizes me in front of staff; intimidating	Emotional security	Badmouthed him

Take a look at the fourth column. Have people done you wrong? Of course. Can you change that? Probably not. You and God are the only team that can transform your perceptions. So keep the focus on you; never mind what others did or didn't do, just focus on your part in the resentment. This is what will give you freedom. You're not letting all these people who have harmed you off the hook by doing this; you're accepting that it may not be up to you to hold them accountable. But you have to evict them from your head and your heart.

Remember, "The truth will set you free. But first, it will piss you off." Your resentment inventory may well uncover patterns of jealousy, envy, bitterness, self-pity, playing the victim, expectations, judgment, blaming, entitlement, dependence, domination, etc.

14. Activity for Chapter Seven

The fear inventory is similar to the resentment inventory. Fear can be dangerous. Many people unconsciously act on their fears. You have to understand your fears to learn what lies behind them. As with the resentment inventory, it helps to get it all down on paper. You may want to look at fear as including concern, worry, or anxiety.

Once your fears are listed, select one to "inventory." Write the name of the fear in the first column. In the next column, write about where the fear comes from or why you have the fear. As an example, let's suppose you fear taking risks. You believe you are in fear of taking risks because "others will judge me."

Fear	Why do I have it/Where does it come from?	Did self-reliance fail me?
Public Speaking	Belief that I am not smart and people will judge me	Yes
Writing a book	People will be highly critical	Yes

The most important part of this process involves taking the risk to trust your Creator and placing the fear in God's hands. As you pray for the fear to be removed, you may ask God to direct your thinking. When this process is put into practice, this translates into courage.

15. Activity for Chapter Seven

A "sex inventory" isn't a list of notches on a bedpost, or a list of conquests, although it can involve a close look back at everyone with whom you have been sexual. However, what you are looking for is not quantity, but quality—specifically the quality you brought to the relationship(s).

Were you manipulative, either using sex to get love or love to get sex? Or was the main quality you brought to the relationship that of jealousy, a feeling of insecurity that made you want to control your partner? As you write the names of your partners and the wrongs you feel they have done you in the column format, take a good look at the last column, and be honest about what your part in the resentment or other relationship problem was. You may find that you have been fearful, selfish, manipulative, or jealous, and I'm willing to bet that's not really the way you want to be in your future relationships. Once you have seen the qualities you don't want to bring to present or future relationships, you are on the road to successfully changing your behavior.

16. Activity for Chapter Seven

At times, looking at fears, resentments, and relationship issues can become discouraging. You need to identify and own your assets because they are part of who you are as much as your deficits. In compiling your asset inventory, feel free to get feedback from friends and family, because often others can see you better than you can see yourself.

Secrets are another important thing to put down on paper, especially things about yourself or your actions that you would rather take to your grave. Secrets are like mushrooms; they thrive in the dark. But you want to live in the light, so secrets have to go. Sharing secrets can be difficult, but with a trusted mentor, you can do it.

Once you've completed your inventories (resentments, fear, sex and secrets), you will move to the next phase of your development.

The whole act of writing out each inventory is an incredibly enlightening process. All it takes is a notebook and pen and some willingness, a prayer at the top of the page and a little guidance from someone who has been through this process him- or herself. You find these people in any twelve-step meeting, but you can also find them in any religious tradition, because moral inventory—no matter what name it goes by—seems to be a universally recognized tool in the process of spiritual healing.

17. Activity for Chapter Eight

It is so important for everyone to have at least one person in his or her life from whom nothing need be kept secret—including thoughts, emotions, past actions, shames, resentments, guilt, fears, secrets, character defects, hopes, dreams, and aspirations. Since most people suffer from the imposter syndrome, we all need someone to know and accept us at our core.

The next task is for you to take your inventory to your mentor, pastor, rabbi, or a trusted and close-mouthed friend who understands the value of confession.

18. Activity for Chapter Nine

Your mentor, especially if he or she has applied these spiritual principles, will listen to why you think you have harmed somebody and then help you with what you need to say to that person. There will be times when you need to wait, or make no direct restitution at all. For instance, in the majority of cases, you should not go to an ex-girlfriend or ex-boyfriend. The complexity of such situations makes this a tricky area, and you should ask your mentor/sponsor for advice if you have questions about this one. You are really not in the best position to determine if another person could be further hurt by your efforts. Check with your sponsor/mentor; examine your own motives, and follow your mentor's advice. Your job is to be willing to go the distance in order to solidify your new life.

19. Activity for Chapter Ten

Growing spiritually means learning to incorporate certain spiritual principles into your daily life. You either just completed or are in the midst of the amends process, in which the focus was on past actions where you caused others hurt. Now you need to learn how to admit—as soon as an offense occurs—that you were wrong, rather than letting hurt and resentments fester and grow. Twelve-step literature tells us to be aware of fear, anger, and any forms of self-hared or self-obsession. We need to ask God for relief as soon as we notice these negative thoughts or emotions. Then we need to strive to "get out of self" by being of service to others.

20. Activity for Chapter Ten

As you grow spiritually, you learn how to accept responsibility for your part in any given situation. Learning how to say "I was wrong" will be extremely helpful in your quest for spiritual connection. Bring your hurts and issues to your spiritual guide, to your spiritual group, and to God. Be willing to look at your part. Ask for guidance on how to deal with each situation. Please learn now that you need to honestly examine your part: own it, accept it, admit it, amend it, and get over it. Eventually, it will become part of your lifestyle and you will ask, "What would my God have me do in this situation?"

21. Activity for Chapter Ten

Do whatever you can to improve your relationships. Don't ever stop learning and growing. There are many good books you can read and techniques you can practice, but the truth is that no book or technique is going to be a panacea when it comes to relationships. The key is to look for what God is saying to you in these relationships and to always be willing to look at yourself first.

22. Activity for Chapter Eleven

If you do nothing else, pray. Whether you believe in God or not—pray. Pray something like, "God—if there is a God—please help me today." Whatever the area of your life in which you need help (which is every area for me), where you need insight, strength, wisdom, or power beyond your own capabilities, it will be of the utmost importance that you pray. Sometimes it is how we pray that makes the difference.

23. Activity for Chapter Eleven

Develop spiritual rituals for yourself. Make time for your relationship with your Higher Power—while out for a walk, or while having your morning coffee.

God speaks to us through the events, the relationships, and circumstances in our lives, so we need to be aware. Where is God in this situation? What is He saying to me through it? Taking time for self-reflection can give us the ability to get the correct perspective on our current situation. We usually can't get perspective when we are in the midst of the "day-to-day," so it is important to set aside some quiet time in a special place in your home that is dedicated to prayer, meditation, and reflection.

24. Activity for Chapter Eleven

Take a word that has sacred meaning for you, like "Jesus," "God," "Life," "Spirit," "Love," or "Peace," and you gently repeat it when you find yourself distracted by thoughts. You need to treat thoughts as if you were window-shopping, not holding on to them in any way. The point is to practice and experience the moments when there is no attachment to any thought or emotion—when there is silence in your inner being. The practice works best when you dedicate twenty minutes twice a day to sit, breathe, and just be. You only understand how valuable meditation is when you stop doing it and find out how much balance, direction, and love it brings.

25. Activity for Chapter Eleven

Memorize a prayer and sit quietly for twenty minutes and say it slowly every day, until it becomes part of your being. Since I follow the twelve-step suggestion to be of service to others, I like to pray, "God, please put me in a position to be of maximum service to you and your children." I have prayed this over and over and the results have been nothing short of miraculous. If your brain resists for fear that all fun will cease when you pray in earnest, you are in for a huge surprise. I know now that God has my healing and happiness in mind and that I am the only obstacle to immense freedom and usefulness.

26. Activity for Chapter Eleven

I practice a form of conversation called the "gratitude game." My wife and I play it in the car and the kids will join in from time to time. It is pretty simple, with as many variations as you like. In the most basic form, you express something that you are grateful for, such as your health, children, home, struggles, challenges, and so on. When you have finished, the next person expresses gratitude. It's hard to be in self-pity and gratitude at the same time. Getting into gratitude is a great way to change your thoughts and feelings, especially when you begin to truly realize that this is all a gift on loan from God. We do not earn any of the amazing gifts we have been given.

27. Activity for Chapter Twelve

The task for this stage of your development is to commit to a couple of hours of service work per week, for six months. I hope that eventually it will become a way of life for you without ego-involvement, because—as many of the sages acknowledge—it is enlightened self-interest. Pray to be used by God even if you are unaware of it. In fact, that would be the best-case scenario, because you'll be in no danger of spiritual pride . . .

What is "it" for you? Are you an addict? Do you struggle with anxiety, depression, obesity, or greed? What were the struggles that made you feel enough pain to read and use this book for personal growth? Pray that God brings people into your life who struggle with the same issues as you do, so that you can reach out and share your story with them. Your story needs to reveal your struggles and the solution of living by spiritual principles. Your life only just began as you stopped living for yourself and started living for what you can contribute. Look for opportunities to serve as an act of self-preservation and out of gratitude for the life you have been given.

28. Chapter Twelve

I hope that you receive the message that you have something to give to others—whether it be your time, your money, your expertise, your prayers, or a combination thereof. The implementation is the hard part, so you need to be of service to someone today in order to get momentum. Pay and commit to some form of service work—and act on it. We all know intellectually what is right, but it is the practice and the living of the ideals that is the hard part.

29. Activity for Chapter Thirteen

Imagine you are ninety years old and on your deathbed. Will certain people surround you? Who are they? Will it be your children, grandchildren, and good friends? How intimate are those relationships? What are you leaving behind for memories? What have you accomplished? Has your work benefitted others? In what ways has your life impacted the community around you? What is your view of death? How is your relationship with God? Were your dreams fulfilled? Did you have integrity? What kind of man or woman have you become? Was your work meaningful? Did it enable

others, like your children, to better themselves? Do you have regrets? Do
you know love? Write all this down.

Ask yourself these questions as if you knew you were to die today, and from
the perspective as if you had been granted many more years to live. Take this
last assignment seriously. Journal as much as you need to and then simplify,
because the time you take to do this exercise will enable you to see the
elements of your life that are extraneous to your life vision—the elements
on which you will want to stop spending time and energy. For instance, you
may find yourself working less because you realize that making a little more
money and impressing your boss and co-workers has no relevance in your
life vision. It may result in your watching far less television, or being more
intentional about the programs you do watch.

30. Activity for Chapter Thirteen

Make a Vision Statement. A way to conceptualize your vision statement
is to think of who you want to become and what you would want to
accomplish (in a perfect world). You need to think big because it is an act of
faith in where God can take you. There is no room for false modesty here.
We need to have an idealized direction. Your mission will describe your
sense of purpose and the qualities you possess that will help you fulfill your
mission. Try to embed your values and priorities into the statement.

31. Activity for Chapter Thirteen

Start writing a hope list for each area of your life, including employment,
family, friends, relationship with God, interests, health/fitness, legacy, impact
on your community or society, work, travel, etc. You can have as many
categories as you wish. Write down what is important to you. Who do you
want to be? Who do you want to love? How do you want to be of service? It
will take you a couple of hours per year even if you do the minimum, and it
will still have a strong impact on your life. Many people will take the time to
visualize their hopes and dreams for ten minutes per day.

Take those lists and start to narrow down the themes and start to prioritize
the importance of each sub-category. Whatever your lists turn out to be,

you can start to condense a lot into a life vision. Ask God for help. Ask a professional for help if you think that will be helpful. A life coach can be very helpful during this process, too.

Think big but take the small actions today that will take you towards the manifestation of your hopes, dreams, and visions. Using a marriage example, it does not matter how you "feel"—give your partner a hug today because that is a small action that you can take towards a loving and healthy marriage or partnership. It is building a lifestyle around the little things— today—that will bring you towards the realization of your larger vision.

Practice the principles conveyed in the chapters of this book and they will completely transform your life. Do not let the good things that God gives you take you away from your primary relationship, which is with God. You will find that doing this provides you with a way of life that is second-to-none.